NEW PERSPECTIVES ON
BREAKING
THE

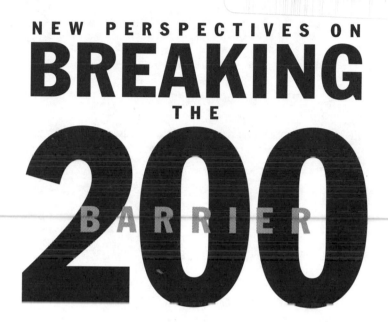

BILL M. SULLIVAN

Beacon Hill Press of Kansas City
Kansas City, Missouri

ISBN 083-412-1786

Printed in the
United States of America

Cover Design: Cristina F. Mershon

Library of Congress Cataloging-in-Publication Data

Sullivan, Bill M.
  New perspectives on breaking the 200 barrier / Bill M. Sullivan.
     p. cm.
  Includes bibliographical references (p.   ).
  ISBN 0-8341-2178-6 (pbk.)
  1. Church growth. I. Title.

  BV652.25.S848 2005
  254'.5—dc22

                                                    2005007101

10   9   8   7   6   5   4   3   2   1

The original version of this book was dedicated to C. Peter Wagner, whose peerless teaching continues to be a strong influence in my life. In this version I wish also to include three of the best religious researchers anywhere—

Dale E. Jones

Kenneth E. Crow

Rich Houscal

who for a quarter century have provided me with outstanding research and wonderful friendship.

CONTENTS

ABOUT THE AUTHOR

BILL M. SULLIVAN began his ministry in 1957 in a home mission church in Denver. His experience in breaking the 200 barrier makes this book more than a theoretical treatise. He led one of his churches through growth from less than 200 to over 700. His dissertation for the D.Min. degree conferred by Fuller Theological Seminary dealt with a church growth strategy he developed and tested.

Dr. Sullivan developed the K-Church Project, including the School of Large Church Management, for pastors desiring to build a great church for the glory of God and the redemption of people. He developed the strategy and authored the book *NewStart—Starting Strong New Churches the Right Way*, which has resulted in a significant increase in the number of new churches started in his denomination. He is also author of *Ten Steps to Breaking the 200 Barrier* and *Churches Starting Churches* and coeditor of *The Smaller Church in a Super Church Era*. He cofounded an association of sociologists of religion, facilitated the development of the Church Growth Research Center, and is active in, and a past president of, the American Society for Church Growth and recipient of the organization's Donald McGavran Church Growth Award. He cofounded *GROW Magazine,* a photo journal of mission and evangelism.

Sullivan was director of the USA/Canada Mission/Evangelism Department for his denomination for 23 years. He currently serves as a seminar speaker and consultant.

A free teacher's lesson preparation kit is available for downloading online at <www.200barrier.org>. Other free resources for understanding and planning to break the 200 barrier are also available online at the same site. A link to the publisher's site is provided for ordering additional multiple copies at a special rate.

FOREWORD

I'm guessing that you're one of many church leaders, perhaps a pastor, who visits bookshops. You pick up one book after another. You leaf through each book for a minute or so. You vaguely recall how many books you've already bought in the past that you haven't yet read. You can't even recall where some of them are! Now, as you peruse this book, you ask, "Should I spring for this book? Can I justify this purchase? Would I prioritize reading this book? If I put its insights into practice, would it make a difference?"

The answer to all of those questions is a definite "Probably!" If your church is *not* one of the 80 percent across the land that are stuck or declining in membership strength, or if your church has plateaued at around 200 in average attendance but you already know how to move past "the 200 barrier" and the other places churches typically get stuck, or if you and your church already have your "apostolic act" to gether, then feel free to take a pass on this book. If, however, the previous sentence does not describe your situation, then buy this book now, even if it means spending your lunch money! You didn't need to "super size them fries" anyway.

Donald McGavran, father of the church growth movement within Christianity's world mission, often observed that church growth is "complex." He meant that if a church is growing (or stagnant or declining), it's due to multiple causes, and some of those causes may not yet be understood. The experience of many churches that have grown to, say, 175 to 225 in worship attendance is as "complex" as any challenge that growing churches and their leaders face. Only a few growing churches have grown to around 200, leveled off for a while, and then figured out all on their own how to break past the barrier and experience new growth, but not many. Most churches at that stage need a "map" to get over this formidable hill.

This book provides such a map. It's an update and revision of the author's earlier *Ten Steps to Breaking the 200 Barrier.* I have met church leaders, especially but not exclusively in the Church of the Nazarene, who rigorously implemented the insights of that book, and their churches planned, made strategic adjustments, reached out in old ways and new, and grew again. Now, supported by more recent research and years of reflection, this edition is destined to help 50,000 churches experience new growth.

You should know that the author, Bill Sullivan, was probably the most effective director of evangelism for any denomination in America in our lifetime. Since I also served in that capacity for my denomination, I would have some basis for that judgment! Now, following his recent retirement, Sullivan has revised and updated his now-classic text. While the first edition was excellent, this edition adds perspective from Sullivan's considerable wisdom.

This edition is not merely an update; it breaks some new ground. Take, for instance, the book's early emphasis upon a congregation's "choice points." Bill Sullivan seems to be trying to sensitize church leaders to the fact that congregations are kind of like people: largely, we become the people (and churches) we are as a result of the choices we once made more or less unconsciously. Sullivan observes that we make better choices when the decision process is conscious rather than unconscious. He wants the early material in this book to ground readers in the art of making conscious, informed decisions about their church's future. If you're harboring the illusion that you're already rooted in this art, then begin your reading at chapter four, and return later to the "choice point" material.

This book even offers new insight in subjects, like prayer and faith, where we don't usually expect new insight. When, on those subjects, Sullivan is reminding us of what we somewhat knew already, he does so in fresh ways. No writer I can recall, for example, has applied Martin Luther's famous line to the spiritual factors that are operative in the growth of churches: "Were not the right Man on our side, our striving would be losing."

The field of church growth, however, is analogous to the field of agriculture. No farmer has a crop to harvest without God's blessing, but agricultural scientists especially study the human role in farming. Church growth, likewise, has human and divine sides, and the church growth scholar's most indispensable contribution comes from studying the human side of church growth. So Sullivan's chapters on planning, implementing, and leading (and on "choice points") may become the most influential.

On the divine-human issue, however, evangelization is not exactly like agriculture. Jesus said that the Father sends His rain upon "the just and the unjust"—so the harvests of "pagan" farmers are often abundant! In apostolic outreach, however, for too many reasons to unpack here, the consecration of church leaders to the Lord of the harvest is essential to the harvest.

—George G. Hunter III, Ph.D.
Professor of Evangelism and Church Growth
Asbury Theological Seminary

PREFACE

Much has changed in the church world since I wrote *Ten Steps to Breaking the 200 Barrier* in 1988. Contemporary worship has changed the preferences of many churches so that resources have to be completely redesigned. Anti-Christian sentiment has escalated at an almost exponential pace. The church and clergy experience a greatly reduced position of respect and appreciation in the community. Radical individualism, so prevalent in the culture, has been flooding into the Church, producing high demands on the clergy and igniting conflict in the fellowship. It's a tough time to be a pastor. It isn't easy being a layperson either!

But to borrow an idea from Charles Dickens, it is the best of times and the worst of times. Opportunities for sharing the Good News abound. People are lost in a meaningless world with little or no idea of what their life is all about. The message of Christ is the best news they could ever hear.

Churches not only *can* grow but *are* growing —and many vigorously. Your church also can rise from its plateau, or even decline, and break through the 200 barrier. For that reason I have prepared *New Perspectives on Breaking the 200 Barrier* and have greatly revised the 10 steps of my 1988 version. The steps are essentially the same, but several chapters have been completely rewritten. The research has been totally restudied, and all the ideas and terminology have been updated. More important, I have had 15 more years of experience, working in my denominational headquarters and studying thousands of churches.

The first three chapters, on choice points, and chapter four, explaining the 200 barrier, are written especially to laypersons. The remainder of the book is directed primarily to the pastor. However, both clergy and laity will profit from studying all the material. Everyone needs to be fully aware of all the challenges involved in breaking the 200 barrier.

I submit this new perspective and greatly revised edition with the prayer that it will give new hope and enable hundreds of pastors to lead their churches in breaking the 200 barrier.

INTRODUCTION
A NEW PERSPECTIVE

Someone has said, "Perspective is how things look from where you are." In the late 1980s the Charles E. Fuller Evangelistic Institute was widely presenting the seminar "Breaking the 200 Barrier." Concurrently in the business world, the literature was reflecting an emphasis on leadership. The "great man" theory was being strongly advocated. "Everything rises and falls on leadership" was the mantra of the times.

At the same time, the church growth movement was at the height of its popularity. Growth of small churches into larger congregations was advocated and resourced with new principles and strategies. The seminar on "Breaking the 200 Barrier" was one of the most popular seminars, if not the most popular, Fuller ever offered.

It was only natural that the thinking on leadership would affect the thinking on breaking the 200 barrier and indeed on all church growth thinking. It was a correct perspective and a very important one. The significance of leadership in church growth should never be minimized. This book does not offer an alternative perspective to the importance of leadership in breaking the 200 barrier. Rather, it sets forth an *additional* perspective on that task—something like the story of the three blind men describing an elephant based on one having hold of the elephant's trunk, another holding its leg, and the third holding its tail. Their descriptions were quite different, but it was the same elephant.

Actually, the Fuller seminar insights about the 200 barrier were quite accurate. Their strategies were appropriate and well devised. A pastor should have been able to utilize them in successfully leading his or her church to break the 200 barrier. Unfortunately, the barrier turned out to stubbornly resist the power of leadership. A few exceptionally gifted pastors were able to lead their churches through the barrier. However, most pastors did not experience such success. In time, the idea of attempting to break the 200 barrier was forgotten.

There was never really much literature about the topic. In 1988 I wrote the book *Ten Steps to Breaking the 200 Barrier.* Carl George wrote the book *How to Break Growth Barriers* in 1993, but it covered four growth barriers, and only 14 pages were dedicated specifically to the 200 barrier. Interestingly, even today, a Google search of the Internet yields only one book on the 200 barrier in the first 50 entries, plus four references to papers or a chapter in a book. During the last 10 years almost nothing on the topic has appeared in publication.

Yet most church growth advocates recognize the challenge of the 200 barrier and typically recommend the *leadership* perspective on breaking the barrier. The purpose of this book is to provide an additional perspective on breaking the barrier—one that sees the *congregation* as critical to success. And this perspective is not merely about mobilizing the laity, although that's an important factor in growth. It's not about goal ownership or "buy-in" by the congregation, though those two aspects are also important to growth.

This book is about *the decisions regarding church size lay leaders and the congregation as a whole make and live by.* It's about tacit assumptions that remain fixed and unresponsive to change. It's about values and preferences and priorities that are widely believed and firmly held. It's about a strategy for dealing with these factors rather than placing the responsibility on pastoral leadership alone. It is recognizing the fact that "the gate of change is locked on the inside."

In the mid-1980s I met with a group of successful pastors of churches in the 200-barrier range to devise a denominational training program to help pastors break the 200 barrier. One of the pastors offered an insight that redirected the thinking of the group. He said, "It isn't just the pastors who need training—it's the people. Unless they understand what is involved in breaking the barrier and are willing to accept the changes and pay the price for growth, there isn't much chance it will happen. Pastors need something that will reinforce the leadership they're attempting to give to the congregation." His observation helped us develop a strategy that provided training material for lay leaders in the local church. Unfortunately, our perspective was still on the leader, and our materials dealt more with pastors and programs than with the laity and congregational culture. This book is an attempt to add the insights of "choice points" to previous perspectives on leadership and build an improved and hopefully more effective strategy for breaking the 200 barrier.

There may be a greater possibility of change if congregations truly understand the issues involved. This is not to say people will change their natural preferences for face-to-face relationships. Neither is it so naive as to suggest lay leaders will charitably surrender their position and control. It's simply a hope that understanding will enable people to transcend their situation and make decisions based on the Great Commission and the challenge of pre-Christian people in the community.

A pastor once told me of a layperson's response to learning about power and control. The man said to his pastor, "The last time our church launched a major growth thrust, I admit that I was the one who opposed and stopped it. I thought I was doing the right thing, but now I realize I kept our church from growing. But, Pastor—I promise that if you will lead us in growth, I will not oppose it, and you will have my full support."

It's that kind of insight and commitment that must be achieved *throughout the congregation* in order to break the 200 barrier. It's with the prayer for that kind of miracle that this book is written.

1
WHAT ARE CHOICE POINTS?

The term "choice points" is not an uncommon term. It's used by computer programmers to indicate a point on a software decision tree. It's used by educators to identify points at which implementation decisions are made. Sociologist Thomas F. O'Dea used the term to tell people who study religious groups that we would do better in trying to understand why movements become bureaucratic institutions if we could identify "dilemmas or choice points which give rise to one kind of organizational tendency rather than another."[1] Sociologist J. Alan Winter identified "dimensions or choice-points facing religious congregations" as they maintain or change their nature.[2] He included issues like

● Membership by birth vs. membership by profession of faith;
● High vs. low member involvement;
● Professional clergy vs. priesthood of all believers;
● Conforming to society vs. tension with society;
● Focus on the masses vs. the classes.[3]

Kenneth E. Crow, a sociologist and also a pastor, missionary, educator, administrator, and now denominational researcher, uses the term to describe

a major area of decision, an issue with significant consequences—even though congregational or denominational leaders would not necessarily recognize the significance or consequences. . . . Decisions made around a choice point (or around the significant issue, or in the significant area) might be conscious and formal, but they are very often not. We seem to drift into decisions [that take us] away from our denominational roots and original mission and may be making us less likely to reach the unreachable people.[4]

Dr. Crow suggests *congregation size* is one of the major choice points congregations face. Sometimes the choice point regarding size comes in the *context* of other issues or dilemmas and often in *contrast* to the more routine decisions congregations make. The decision regarding congregational size may be made unconsciously and will tend to become part of the congregational culture. It will not be casually or easily changed. If for some reason the congregation is forced to reconsider its decision because of a demographic change or church crisis or some similar event, the decision may be reaffirmed or changed. If the decision is reaffirmed, another layer is added to the culture of the congregation; if the decision is changed, the history of the church takes another direction.

People may make decisions regarding congregation size that are not overt, formal decisions. In fact, most are informal decisions and sometimes unconscious ones. Interestingly, the conclusions are widely accepted and firmly held. Once these decisions are made, congregations appear to cycle up and down within the size range allowed by the organizational issues of the choice point. These decisions tend to prevent losses that would cause them to decline below the chosen range, and they resist additions that would move them significantly above that range.

The congregation size choice point is of great significance because of the implications of the Great Commission. Christ's commission is binding on all Christians and all Christian congregations. It is not possible for a congregation to obey the Great Commission without facing the issue of church size. It may decide to break through the 200 barrier, or it may decide to remain the same size and sponsor a new church periodically. Either decision involves obedience to the Great Commission. [5]

Dr. Crow's way of thinking about church size may prove to be a breakthrough in church growth theory, for it provides a way for churches to understand how choice points, perhaps even more than pastoral leadership and/or organizational structures, determine the size of their congregation. It would be helpful in many churches to be able to bring to the surface the latent existing decisions about size. It would make possible the development of more comprehensive and effective strategies for breaking the 200 barrier. Undoubtedly, thousands of congregations would reverse their decisions and make new ones to break through the 200 barrier and win hundreds of people in their communities to Christ.

It may be an over-simplification to state that choice points, as we use the term, may be *occasions when people make decisions about factors that determine their congregation size*. Even so, this concise definition may enable us to readily work through the complexity of determinants of church size.

Choice points may be *points in time* when a formal or informal, and sometimes unconscious, decision is made regarding a value, preference, attitude, or response. Sometimes these choice points are marked by an *opportunity*, like a rapid population increase in the community. A *crisis*, like the church building burning, may confront the congregation with a decision of whether to relocate to reach a younger community or simply rebuild in the same location to preserve a valued tradition. Choice points may also come from *events*, such as the success of a community program. Instinctive responses in these situations often become decisions with long-term consequences. They add another layer of assumptions to the history and culture of the congregation.

Choice points arise around *issues*. The need to hire additional staff may press the congregation to think about the kind of financial responsibility they want to assume or the kind of relationship with the pastor they want to preserve. A community need may challenge the church to decide whether they will be outwardly focused or inwardly preoccupied. Failure to respond to the need will, in fact, be a decision in favor of continuing as an inwardly focused fellowship.

Congregations face choices fairly consistently regarding matters of *preference*. Musical taste, style of worship, emotional comfort, décor and color preference, and exposure or anonymity frequently become points in which subtle decisions are made that both form and express a congregational personality.

Challenge and risk also force choice points on congregations. Is the congregation willing to grow, accept new people, build a larger building, or even relocate? How heavy of a financial responsibility is the congregation willing to assume? Are the people willing to attempt a worthwhile community project that might fail and embarrass them with their non-church friends? Is the culture of the congregation to always "play it safe"?

These descriptions only begin to sketch out the dimensions of congregational beliefs, values, attitudes, feelings, and preferences. Every choice point in one way or another challenges these factors of congregational life and personality. In the next chapter we will consider some common dilemmas or tensions that call for decisions that tend to determine congregation size.

2
COMMON CHOICE POINTS

Not only individuals but organizations regularly face decisions that determine their future. Just as with individuals, some of the decisions organizations must make have serious and far-reaching consequences. The decisions most difficult to manage are the ones made without even knowing they were made.

Congregational meetings of churches are known for both the ease and the difficulty with which decisions are made. Some members complain they're only a rubber stamp for the pastor's plans. Others impatiently suffer while members haggle for hours over some insignificant agenda item. Quite apart from the congregational meeting, or even a church board meeting, congregations make decisions from time to time, and over a period of time, of which they're unaware. Unfortunately, some of these decisions have powerful and long-term consequences. Sometimes one of the decisions is a choice point that restricts growth and prevents them from breaking the 200 barrier. In this chapter we will examine in a fairly general way some of the more common choice points churches face.

■ THE ACTION-VS.-INERTIA CHOICE POINT ■

Action may be the key to success in most fields of endeavor. Intelligence, talent, and even skill may not keep pace with the hugely successful strength of action. Someone has said, "Starting—the job's half done." Thinking, planning, detailing, and, yes, praying have an important place. But the human aspect of the task never gets done until someone begins to act.

Few people are opposed to action. Most everyone understands it's essential to accomplishment. Not many tasks go undone because people don't think they need to be done. No, the reason worthwhile tasks never get accomplished is that no one ever takes action on them.

It's always easier not to take on a new task. The things we're already doing have expanded to fill all of our available time. It would require a reordering of our priorities to accept another responsibility. In order to take on another program, churches would have to revise their schedules, maybe reallocate the use of space, recruit additional workers, and perhaps raise extra money. And besides, they like things the way they are.

Action always produces some level of change, and that creates discomfort—even pain. A woman hung the motto "Prayer Changes Things" in her kitchen. A few days later it was missing. She asked her husband if he knew what happened to it. "I took it down," he said.

His wife was astounded. "Don't you believe in prayer?" she asked.

"Of course I do," her husband replied. "I just don't like *change*—so I took it down."

Variety may be the spice of life, but it's easy to get too much pepper in the porridge. A little change is acceptable, but significant change is disturbing. It forces people out of their routine into new practices and purposes.

This preference for the routine may be the result of considering the mission of the church less important than the social relationships in the church. The primary concern is that friendship groups are maintained and congregational harmony is preserved. If those are in place, then don't rock the boat.

The Great Commission cannot tolerate any priority above mission. Social relationships are a vital factor in the ministry and mission of the Church, but they *serve* the mission—they must never replace it. Church growth research has revealed how friendships and relationships are the "bridges of God."[1] It's across these bridges that people come to the church and to faith in Christ. But the means (relationships) must never replace the end (mission). Unfortunately, that's what has happened in most small churches!

Small churches are quite effective in conservation. They replace their losses through *biological growth* (the children of members) and transfers from other churches. Their priority on relationships sometimes attracts an occasional visitor, but their preoccupation with their own friends excludes more people than it attracts.

Churches confront the choice point of "action vs. inertia" in a variety of ways:

- The implications of the Great Commission and similar biblical passages.
- Sermons that challenge Christians to be active in ministry and witness to the world.
- Opportunities to reach people experiencing acute need.
- The call to actively support the effort to grow and break through the 200 barrier.

Sermons on the Great Commission and the reality of needy people in the community are easy to forget—"out of sight (or sound), out of mind." Christians usually agree with the sermons they hear and feel compassion for people in need. Unfortunately, they seldom take action.

How long would it take to win the whole world to Christ if every Christian won just one new person to Christ each year? How many people would visit the church if every member invited just one person a month? How many needs could be met if every Christian helped just one person a year? These are theoretical questions, but they have profound practical possibilities.

Feeling guilty doesn't help. A preacher friend of mine told me about a church he pastored for a while in a small community. Once when he had preached a sermon that laid a lot of guilt on the people, a dear lady shook his hand at the door and said, "I just love it when you preach like that. It makes me feel so bad." Such feeling seldom motivates to action. It may only inoculate a person against deep, powerful, feelings that might motivate to action.

Action should be more than activity. It needs to be growth-producing action. A church attempting to break the 200 barrier will need to focus action on activities that bring people to church and to Christ. Breaking out of malaise and inviting family, friends, and associates to church is highly productive action. Intensifying your praying and interceding for specific people to come to faith is powerful action. Organizing and leading recovery groups is also effective growth action.

Far too many churches never break the 200 barrier because of the inertial force of inactivity.

■ THE COMFORT-VS.-DISCOMFORT CHOICE POINT ■

There are specific *places* we feel very relaxed and calm. Certain *practices* are easy for us. We're comfortable with people we've known for an extended period of time. We enjoy being together with friends at church, in one of their homes, or at an outing. Conversation comes easily. We've shared many experiences across the years. We're aware of their likes and dislikes, their strengths and weaknesses. And we understand that they know all about us. It's a good feeling of mutuality.

Put us with people we don't know and expect us to converse about more than the weather, and we suddenly become very uncomfortable. Send us to a place we've never been, and we become tense and apprehensive. Ask us to do something we're not accustomed to doing, and we'll use almost any excuse to avoid doing it.

We have comfort zones. A place may be a *physical* comfort zone. Certain people provide our *social* comfort zone. A familiar practice is our *personal* comfort zone. When we move out of any of our comfort zones, we experience discomfort. We'll usually do most anything to avoid getting out of our comfort zones.

People take their comfort zones with them to church. They're comfortable in their own classroom and in their favorite pew in the sanctuary. It's easy for them to visit with people they know quite well. Singing, praying, and participating in worship in various ways are familiar practices to them. In short, at church they're in their comfort zone.

Visitors represent intrusions into church attendees' comfort zones. Because visitors are guests, regular attendees feel some obligation to serve as host to them. But that requires them to move out of their social comfort zone. A few people find this easy, but most do not. A tension rises between graciousness and timidity. Most of the time timidity paralyzes them in their comfort zone. When a large majority of the people in the congregation respond this way, a church feels unfriendly—and actually is!

How will a congregation respond to visitors? The decision isn't made by public vote—it's made by default. People aren't even conscious they've made a decision—but they have! They've faced a choice point. They've decided it's better to ignore the visitor than to move out of their social comfort zone for the sake of the Great Commission and the evangelistic outreach of the church.

The comfort-vs.-discomfort choice point differs from the action-vs.-inertia choice point not because comfort is *easier* but because it's *preferable*. As such, it represents, not an omission, but a *commission* of inappropriate commitment. A preference for ease may respond to the choice point with inaction, but that's not its essence. Its essence is a misplaced value and will normally respond in a way that preserves and prioritizes comfort for its own sake.

There is probably no more growth-restricting behavior for a congregation than the unwillingness to move out of its comfort zones.

■ THE CONTROL-VS.-RELEASE CHOICE POINT ■

The desire for control is buried deep in the DNA of human beings. It expresses itself first in a person's insistence on controlling his or her own life. It moves quite naturally to an inclination to control other people. Of course, there's variety in human personality, and not everyone seems equally inclined toward controlling other people. But that may be more a result of circumstance than of nature. Often a person who shows no tendency whatsoever toward controlling other people becomes very controlling when given the opportunity. The people who are most negative about someone controlling other people often become "control freaks" when they come into power. There may be people who have no desire for control, but they're closer to being the exception than they are to being the rule.

Control expresses itself in many ways in the church. Some people are elected to positions of service and leadership. Many people are selected for various responsibilities. A measure of control is implicit in these positions. A few people are given control because of their influence. They may be some of the original founders of the church or descendants of the founding family. They may be wealthy or people of stature in the community. They may simply be wise or socially esteemed. In any event, they possess the power to control others by their influence.

Many churches have a small group of persons who hold enormous sway over the life and operation of the church, often called the "power structure." This is not a formal committee, but it might as well be. Their meetings are not on the church calendar, but they occur just the same—in the vestibule, the parking lot, a restaurant, a home, or wherever the group happens to be together with opportunity to talk privately. Generally, their intentions are pure and they have the best interests of the church at heart. But their conversations result in controlling the direction of the church.

Both clergy and elected lay leaders have positional control. The literature on leadership often denigrates this type of power. And unquestionably, it's not as powerful as leadership that's earned. But persons in positions are granted power to control, especially in times of organizational tranquillity. In many churches this turns out to be a major portion of the time. So the power of position should never be underestimated.

Earned or granted, control has colossal effect on what the church is and does. Control regulates the flow of congregational energy, the expenditure of financial resources, and the response to opportunity and possibilities. While control is necessary to preserve and direct the church and its programs, it easily and quickly migrates to restricting and misdirecting the church. Capable people are held at arm's length by leaders who will not share responsibility or performance with them. New people are forced to wait unreasonably long periods before they're accepted and trusted with responsibility and often are never fully accepted. Aggressive plans for growth are sabotaged behind the scenes. Instead of releasing control and allowing new leaders to emerge, control is retained. Instead of allowing growth efforts to flourish, they're restricted and disparaged.

Decisions to retain control are seldom made by a formal vote—they're usually made informally as people maintain their loyalty to friends and traditional patterns of control. The result is that the church settles into the size level consistent with the controllers' preferences and capabilities.

■ THE CONSERVATIVE-VS.-PROGRESSIVE ■ CHOICE POINT

Balance is a healthy condition. Dynamic tension can be productive. Both conservative and progressive viewpoints have a place in the church. It's not unusual for a church to be comprised of approximately equal numbers of each position. This is a condition that tends to keep a congregation on an even keel.

People who espouse a progressive position want the church to grow in quantity and improve in quality. They favor most progressive efforts that are consistent with Christian theology and ethics. Conservatives want to evaluate every factor in the life of the church. They're constitutionally opposed to "jumping in too soon." It's not wise, and it might be disastrous, they conjecture. These people are not opposed to progress—they just don't want to do anything that hasn't been fully considered.

The progressives have led some churches prematurely into

activities that failed and disappointed the people. Not only that, they seem to discount the failure and hasten to new adventures. Conservatives have wisely held the church back from folly. Unfortunately, they have also prevented the church from realizing a brighter future. Progress isn't made without envisioning a wonderful future and taking the risks necessary to realize that prospect.

Smaller churches tend to be controlled by the conservative perspective because of limited funds and crises they've faced in the past. It's a vicious circle of defeat. Past circumstances have made them very cautious. Their caution makes them unduly conservative. Failure to take the risks necessary for significant progress has left them small and resource-poor, which only reinforces their cautious conservatism. This reality has much to do with the fact that so many churches never break the 200 barrier.

■ THE PARTICIPANT-VS.-SPECTATOR ■ CHOICE POINT

The percentage of active participants in the life and ministry of a church may be one of the most accurate indicators of congregational vitality. It may also point to the growth potential of the church. Everything from musicians, teachers, and greeters to helpers, visitors, and cooks depends on volunteer participation. If a church has a high percentage of participants, they have a greater potential for growth generally and for breaking the 200 barrier specifically.

It isn't clear why some churches have a high percentage of participants and other churches have a low percentage. Obviously there was no congregational vote on the matter. Probably no one remembers any reason their church has many or few participants. It just happened. It may be some congregations have a high percentage of people who are participants because they have a significant number of "join-ers." Or it may simply be that the church has done a better job of recruiting and caring for volunteers.

The effort to break the 200 barrier will require a large number of participants. Spectators will have to be recruited, trained, and assigned to various responsibilities. The success of the effort depends on it.

■ THE CLERGY-VS.-LAITY CHOICE POINT ■

Churches decide if the clergy will be their chaplain or if the entire laity will be ministers. It's a decision of great significance.

Many churches consider the pastor an employee the congregation has engaged to be their chaplain and to care for the religious activities of the church. As such, the pastor is always an outsider, similar to an employee in a family-owned-and-operated business. It's difficult for the pastor to give growth leadership when he or she is viewed by the congregation as a chaplain.

But this perspective has more serious consequences. The most detrimental aspect of the pastor being considered chaplain is that the laity don't perceive ministry to be their responsibility. The New Testament Church had no professional clergy. It was around a century before the professional clergy emerged. *Everyone* was a minister. In time the needs of the expanding Church seemed to demand a professional ministry. Organizational complexity, especially in larger churches, requires specially trained and paid personnel. Clergy, adequately prepared to preserve the doctrinal purity of the church, are necessary. But ministry must remain the responsibility of *all* Christians.

It's difficult to determine when a church decides who will "own" ministry. It can't be found in the minutes of the congregation or board meetings. It was an informal and unconscious decision but has had a profound impact on determining the size of the church.

The church always grows most effectively when the laity is extensively engaged in ministry. In order to break the 200 barrier, lay ministry will need to become a high priority.

These are some of the common choice points congregations face. Undoubtedly, there are many more, perhaps some with more serious growth consequences than these. The ability to break the 200 barrier will come from reevaluating decisions that may have resulted in a growth-restricting congregational culture. The congregation as a whole must be growth-oriented.

3
A CHOICE POINT GROWTH STRATEGY

It's important to understand that the issues we're calling choice points have been known all along. In a seminar on breaking the 200 barrier John Maxwell began his presentation with the topic "Developing the Type of Leadership *and Congregation* Needed to Break the 200 Barrier" (emphasis added). He dealt with commitment, enthusiasm, change, and involvement.[1]

The lack of widespread effectiveness of *the organizational and leadership strategy* for breaking the barrier is not due to the leadership's being unaware of these challenges. The weakness of the strategy is in not sufficiently explaining the intractable nature of these issues and the procedures necessary to reverse their harmful effects.

A strategy for breaking the 200 barrier based on choice points must focus on the congregation and their ability to acknowledge, confront, and make new decisions regarding these issues. The people must be educated in choice point theory and trained in how to face choice points effectively for the accomplishment of the Great Commission.

I have hope that a careful and extended *educational process* may make it possible to bring the subconscious decisions restricting growth into alignment with the overt affirmations for growth. The educational process must be carefully developed and directed. Since it will deal with the group's high priority on face-to-face relationships, it will have the potential for emotional reactions. This must be delicately managed.

Group discussions will be essential to congregational learning. Discussion should not be limited to formal settings but must occur in a variety of informal meetings. Casual discussion should be planned to be part of the process. The process should be understood as ongoing until the church is well over 300 in attendance—perhaps even 500.

The curriculum for the educational process should contain sections on the choice points listed in the previous chapter, as well as other choice points perceived by the people. The idea of a curriculum should not imply only formal teaching settings. Instruction should be incorporated in sermons, referenced in organizational meetings, distributed in printed materials, displayed on bulletin boards, and encouraged and facilitated in individual conversations.

The goal of the educational process would be to bring together the people's outward assertions of wanting the church to grow with their inward growth-restricting inclinations, in an effort to develop a growth-encouraging congregational culture.

If at all possible, lay leaders should be used to teach the concepts to the people and to lead the discussions. The pastor will need to train the lay leaders extensively before they begin teaching the congregation. Superficial explanations of choice point issues will not be adequate. In-depth consideration will be necessary.

The strategy should also include *modeling*. People need to see someone else overcoming the negative aspects of choice points. Laypersons who make significant progress can serve as models for other laypersons. This will reinforce the educational instruction with practical application. For example, laypersons who overcome an average level of timidity can be great encouragement to others in the congregation to move out in welcoming visitors. People who have previously been spectators but have become participants can effectively appeal to others for increased involvement.

Mentoring to develop highly effective lay ministry and witness should be incorporated into the strategy. Models are helpful, but mentors are much more effective. Mentoring is difficult to orchestrate. It usually just happens. But leaders can advocate it and facilitate it by consistently giving it a high level of visibility. Many books on mentoring are available. Circulate them among the highest achievers and those who are observed helping others learn. A seminar on mentoring might be helpful. Use your imagination to think of ways to jump-start mentoring in the congregation.

Structuring the organization to deploy people in changes and activities that help the church break through the 200 barrier will be important to the process. Develop ministries, programs, and activities designed to help people become involved in the process of change and growth.

Implementing will also be crucial to the process. Increase action by setting dates for people to take specific action. Everyone could be asked to take action based on doing something that would help the church grow. Publicize the date for beginning, and give it high visibility. Ask the pastor to make it clear to the congregation this is part of the effort to reevaluate the decisions made at past choice points. Generate as much excitement as possible about people taking definite action on a specific date.

Provide training to help people move out of their social comfort zone. Most people are at least mildly timid. Help them understand the fear that generates timidity and how it's dispelled by moving out of their comfort zone. Perhaps the pastor could preach a sermon on 2 Tim. 1:7—"For God did not give us a spirit of timidity, but a spirit of power, of love and of self-discipline." In a public service, interview people who have overcome a measure of their timidity.

Train leaders to delegate, and encourage them in developing other leaders. Recognize those who are effective in delegating and releasing people for ministry. Give serious consideration to ways you can release control of whatever you may be responsible for, and develop someone else as a leader.

Take note of every step of progress, and report it to people who can circulate it on the "grapevine," or official publication pieces. The pastor should make certain the congregation is aware of the successful progressive efforts of the church. This is a sensitive matter, because the intent should not be to belittle conservative people. The idea is only to encourage the faith of the people to be adventurous for God and the church.

Have an involvement audit performed to determine how many people are actually participating in the ministry of the church. Then set a goal to increase participation by a specific amount in a set time frame. Encourage participation by offering spiritual gifts training. Follow up with interviews and recruitment. As much as possible, deploy people in assignments that actually produce growth. Celebrate the increase in involvement.

Strive to increase lay involvement in ministry. Create a ministry flowchart showing all the lay volunteers who work in the various ministries. Work to staff all the ministries of the church with lay ministers. Pay particular attention to the job description of the pastor, and relieve him or her of as many ministries as possible. It's not so the pastor will have nothing to do but preach—rather, it's to recover the New Testament model of lay ministry.

Be sure to prioritize evangelism. Churches grow most effectively by winning people to the church and to Christ. Keep a record of the new converts. Unless people are regularly being converted, consider reworking the program of the church. There are many ways to evangelize; however, most people come to faith through the invitation of a family member, a friend, or an associate. Encourage invitation evangelism, and be sure to have in place methods that engage first-time visitors.

The strategy for dealing with choice points involves a complete educational process. It also requires leadership and organizational changes that will facilitate growth. Most of all, it requires a focus on choice point issues and an understanding of the extreme difficulty in dealing with them. Because every church is in some ways unique, the strategy will have to be implemented in keeping with those distinctions.

The choice point strategy should include the organizational and leadership strategy and be structured around the 10 steps to breaking the 200 barrier discussed later in this book. In terms of sequence, the pastor should begin with the Introduction and then go to chapter 5 ("Spiritual Preparations"), chapter 8 ("Leading"), and the Conclusion. If the church has any paid or volunteer staff persons, take them through a discussion of the entire book. Then begin working with a group of lay leaders. Be very careful in the selection of this group. There are two qualifications necessary for these people: (1) they should be the most competent lay leaders you have in the congregation, and (2) they should be sufficiently respected by the congregation to be able to lead the people in making significant change.

Teach this group the Introduction and chapters 1-4. Use other books on specific issues to supplement the material in this book. Don't rush this process. Make certain each layperson has a full understanding of choice point theory and the common choice points discussed in chapter 2. Also, teach them about the 200 barrier discussed in chapter 4, and give them an overview of how the church plans to break the 200 barrier.

When—and only when—the lay leaders are trained to the point that they can teach and lead discussions about choice points, begin the process of educating the entire congregation. Choice points perceived to be the primary problems for a particular congregation should be given major attention. This process should be ongoing until attendance is well into the 300-350 range.

At about the same time the education process begins with the entire congregation, the pastor and staff should proceed with chapter 6, on planning, and chapter 7, on implementation. All through the process, keep the focus on the congregation, and help them to deal with choice points. They'll need to reverse some decisions they've made in the past and will need to make Great Commission decisions in the future.

Never underestimate the power of congregational culture. Similar to the bumper sticker motto "Don't Mess with Texas," paste a mental sticker in your mind with the motto "Don't Underestimate the Power of Culture!" It will help you persevere in the task. It will also help you keep your focus on the congregation.

Leadership is important in every aspect of ministry, but congregational culture is crucial in attempting to break the 200 barrier. Thus, this choice point strategy is focused on the congregation rather than the pastor.

In the following chapters we will consider the 200 barrier and 10 steps the church can take in an effort to break the barrier.

4
THE 200 BARRIER

The 200 barrier is the difficulty churches experience in attempting to change from an *association* of friends to an *organization* of worshippers as they grow from below 200 to above 350 in worship attendance.

Until recent years, worship attendance data was not widely available. Since worship attendance is now widely regarded as the most accurate indicator of strength, many churches have begun recording and reporting their attendance statistics. Rich Houseal, president of the Association of Statisticians of American Religious Bodies, discovered a remarkable fact about church sizes based on attendance. The percentage of churches of a particular size is essentially the same for most, if not all, Protestant denominations. His study revealed what many have believed for years— most churches are small, especially when based on worship attendance.

It's not just small denominations that have little churches on the back streets. Small churches are characteristic of all Protestant denominations. The Southern Baptist Convention, with 42,000 churches, and the Assemblies of God, with 12,000 churches, both report between 20 and 25 percent of their churches averaging between 25 and 50 at worship attendance. The same is true for the Presbyterian Church (USA) and several other major and minor denominations. The data are *reports* from denominational offices, not *projections* from survey data.

COMPARISON OF CHURCH WORSHIP ATTENDANCE SIZES BY DENOMINATION: USA 2000

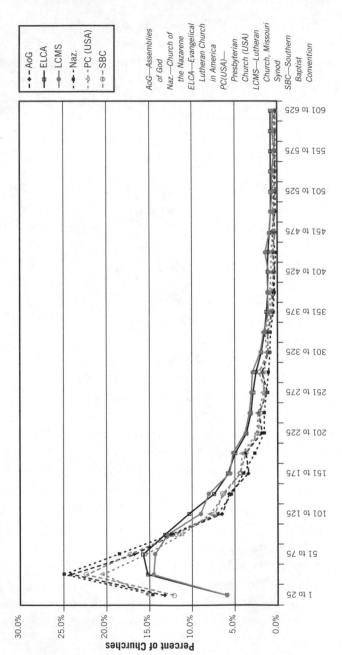

Why are there so many small churches? Does God prefer small churches? If we interpret church attendance statistics the way sociologists generally interpret research projects, we'll conclude the need to have small churches, because that's what we have the most of. That's what people appear to prefer. To paraphrase Abraham Lincoln's famous statement about common people, God must love small churches—because He made so many of them.

The prevalence of small churches and the similarity in size categories among denominations incites us to give special consideration to the factors that restrict attendance growth in small churches.

Only one growth barrier can be discerned from statistical reports of church attendance. One-third to one-half of all churches average fewer than 50 in worship attendance. It appears the 50 barrier is the first and only statistical growth restriction that many churches encounter.

Many reasons can be given for the tendency of churches to remain small. Limited leadership, vision, and resources usually top the list. But other factors such as group characteristics and relational preferences are also cited. The complete list is long.

A small church is not a microcosm of a large church but a totally different kind of organization. Just as you would not want to change from being the person you are to being someone else, neither does a small church want to give up the family atmosphere to become a complex organization. As a matter of fact, the very term has an unfriendly sound.

While statistics provide a valuable perspective on growth, they don't tell the whole story. Statistics do not reveal a growth barrier in the range of 200. Rich Houseal has juxtaposed the statistical reports of churches in a variety of ways and found no indication of a statistical 200 barrier. Yet many church growth advocates remain convinced of a severe growth restriction in the 150-to-350 range. It's perhaps more accurate to speak of the barrier as a range, although most church growth authorities refer to it simply as the 200 barrier. If a single arbitrary figure is to be chosen, then 200 is probably a good selection, since it's more descriptive to speak of the 200 barrier than a barrier range. Those who have spoken and written about the 200 barrier describe it in *relational* and *organizational* terms rather than statistical.

Most people appear to prefer the intimacy, security, and accountability of small-group relationships, and they resist organizational structures and practices that work against that preference. In a small church everyone knows everyone else by name, face, and many other characteristics. As a church increases in size, it becomes increasingly difficult to know everyone.

Some sociologists tend to think a typical person can know only approximately 100 to 150 people. This is consistent with the experience of pastors who say they began to encounter a barrier when attendance reached that amount. In *The Tipping Point* Malcolm Gladwell describes a scientific study that may indicate a biological reason for this limitation. Gladwell also describes "the rule of 150," which further supports the idea of a growth barrier in this range.[1]

While the statistics don't indicate a 200 barrier, nothing in the statistics contradicts the existence of a relational and organizational barrier in the range of 200. Indeed, a very small percentage of churches are larger than 350—the point at which some church growth advocates consider the barrier broken.

Since there is strong indication that a growth barrier prevents most churches from growing to and beyond 200, it would seem a strategy for breaking the barrier would be highly desirable.

An emphasis on organizational barriers emerged in the mid-1980s and has been the primary framework for devising barrier-breaking strategies. However, there isn't much evidence the organizational strategy has been effective in enabling churches to grow through the 200 barrier. Perhaps existing strategies can be improved by helping congregations respond to "choice points" with Great Commission consciousness rather than subconscious restrictive cultural preferences. This may enable thousands of churches to break through the growth barriers of small congregations.

In order for a church to grow from approximately 100 to over 350, a fundamental change in the church will be necessary. The change will be from a *fellowship,* in which everyone in the congregation knows everyone else, to *a corporate-type organization,* in which fellowship and relationships are experienced in subunits of the church.

Another highly significant change will be the relationship between pastor and people. In a small church the people can have direct contact with the pastor. In a large church frequent contact with the pastor is limited to a select few.

Still another consequence of such growth will be the vesting of leadership in the pastor and staff rather than lay leaders. Operation of the church will move from the church board to the executive staff.

These changes will affect both people and pastor. The people will have to give up their control of the church and modify their fellowship within the church. This is the price of growth the people will have to pay!

There's also a high price for the pastor to pay. He or she will have to give up his or her close relationship with the people and learn how to give leadership to a corporate-type church. Lyle Schaller drew the classic comparison when he likened it to the change from being a shepherd to being a rancher. A shepherd has a flock of sheep that he or she tends. A rancher has many flocks for which he or she is responsible. The rancher's care for them is not direct but is carried out through other workers. He or she sees that all the flocks are shepherded, but the rancher is not the person who is the shepherd to each of the sheep.

These changes result in a church that's highly structured and proliferated. It requires a higher level of leadership competency and a more structured approach to the management of the church. Many pastors are either unable or unwilling to fill such a role, in which cases the churches do not grow through the barrier.

A pastor speaking at the 75th anniversary of a church recalled a time in the growth history of the congregation that they began to complain about feeling like strangers because of all the new people. The pastor indicated that this anxiety occurred when attendance was between 200 and 300. But beyond 350 he no longer heard much complaint, because by then they had made the adjustments that resulted in being a totally different kind of church. That was the result of moving from "one big happy family" (with the intimacy and security that comes from being small enough to watch out for each other and take care of each other) to an *organization.* Resistance to this change is the most fundamental aspect of the 200 barrier.

But this raises a question. Is it *desirable* to try to break through the 200 barrier? Several factors must be considered when facing that challenge. What is the demographic situation of the community? A community of 1,500 to 3,000 people, or even 10,000 people, that's static or declining and is adequately churched may not be the best place to try to break the barrier. This is something each church must decide. What is the average-size church in your town? In the thinking of the people, what number constitutes average size?

A pastor must also consider how long he or she plans to stay at the church. If the church increases to 350 and the pastor moves, will the successor allow it to decline back below the barrier?

Still another consideration is the kind of debt commitment that significant growth will require.

The desirability of breaking the barrier also hinges on the question "Do people prefer larger churches?" Today the preference for larger churches seems greater than in the past, though it may not be possible to accurately determine the preferences of the past. Television has exposed people to megachurches. The anonymity of society in general may have caused people to prefer larger groups rather than smaller ones, where accountability is greater.

However, bear in mind that any church that grows larger and sustains growth and at the same time ministers to its people will have within it small accountability groups. A large proportion of the people will be absorbed into some type of group. So people don't escape accountability when they attend a larger church—their accountability is merely organized differently. Of course, larger churches contain many people who are simply spectators, but churches of 60 or 70 also have spectators, though the number may be smaller.

Another factor to consider in deciding whether or not to break the 200 barrier is the desirability of starting a *new church*. Would it not be better to make plans for another church or even several other churches over a period of time? Could the people be served better this way? Could they maintain the intimacy, security, and accountability of the smaller church and still experience the excitement of growth?

Actually, this is not an either/or situation. Sponsoring a

new church generally creates missional enthusiasm and results in the growth of the sponsoring church.

Ultimately, the decision on whether or not to attempt to break the 200 barrier depends not on the desirability of breaking the barrier but on the congregation's response to the Great Commission. How they understand Christ's call for commitment should determine their decision about congregational size.

We will next take a look at the steps congregations must take in breaking the 200 barrier.

5
SPIRITUAL PREPARATIONS

■ STEP 1 ■
EXAMINE YOUR MOTIVE

Why do you want to break the 200 barrier? Unless the motive for growth is to proclaim the Good News to those who are lost (Luke 19:10) and help them become fully devoted followers of Christ, you will be working from an inadequate motive.

Does the motivation come from a desire to pastor a larger church? If so, you have a really big job on your hands. Even if you're an exceptionally gifted and winsome person, with that motive you're going to have a difficult time making a church grow. Undoubtedly it has happened; probably there are some places it's happening right now, and it will likely happen in the future, but that's not the best motivation for growth.

Someone may say, "You're simply advocating a spiritual motivation in order to grow, but growing a large church is still what you want to do. The motivation is still impure." Certainly the motivation should not be simply to grow a larger church. The motivation must always be to obey God's call to make disciples everywhere. There's no such thing as having a vision for the lost in your town only. The assignment that Christ gave to His followers was to reach the whole world. Start at Jerusalem, but don't stop there; work outward. The pastor who wants only to reach his or her local community or city does not really have the mission perspective of a true disciple. This is undoubtedly why many megachurch pastors are starting new churches here in North America as well as in other regions of the world.

This is not promotion for overseas mission; it's a realistic appraisal of the Great Commission. We don't like to believe people are lost. It would be more comfortable to be a universalist, and that would certainly reduce our responsibility. But the Bible will not permit that. It prevents us from believing everyone is going to be saved someday, someway, and it's very plain in declaring that some people will be lost. The sobering message of the Bible is that those who are sent to preach will be held responsible if they fail to warn the lost. Therefore, thinking about breaking the 200 barrier forces us to ask ourselves, *Why do we want to break it? So we can have more people?* That may be good, but that's not a strong-enough motivation.

Motive has not been properly dealt with until the difficulty of being objective is considered. It's too easy to question the motive of another, but actually it's impossible to know his or her thoughts. This is certainly true in regard to growth. One pastor may seek growth in the church and claim it's because he or she wants to see souls saved. Another, looking on, may declare that the pastor simply has a desire for personal advancement. It's well-nigh impossible to determine which person is correct. Even when a person prays searchingly, it's difficult for such a one to know his or her own heart. Most of us have experienced times when we believed we were doing what was right but later wondered if we were carried away under the emotion of the moment. Religious experience and spiritual intimacy are wonderful, but they must always be subjected to the judgment of the Word of God.

The natural tendency of the human heart is to cover up any inclination that might be considered selfish. We use a variety of rationalizations to escape responsibility for impure motives.

People may say, "You're just trying to feather your own nest," or "You're just trying to get your name in the district newsletter," or "You're just trying to build a larger church so you can get a bigger salary." If your motivation is reaching the lost, those kinds of charges will roll off you like water off a duck's back, because you know in your soul that you're seeking the lost.

It's easy to be superficial in the area of motives, just as it's easy to be superficial in the areas of action. Pacifism and inactivity don't necessarily indicate pure motivation, nor does aggressive, energetic action necessarily indicate selfish ambition. We must not allow either Satan or well-intentioned people to cause us to shrink back from being aggressive evangels for Christ. At the same time, we must not allow the desire for personal satisfaction and ambitious fulfillment to be the driving motivation of our ministry.

We say to young people with a call to ministry, "If you can do anything other than preach, then don't preach. But if you have to preach to save your soul, then preach." That's the only kind of conviction that will hold you steady in the ministry when the going gets rough. The realization that we're responsible for the souls of men and women, boys and girls, will keep us going when we run into resistance to growth.

Now, suppose you privately conclude in searching your soul that the truth is that you want to pastor a large church. The truth is, you want to be in the top 10, or the top whatever. You don't want to feel that way about it, but God help you— that's the way you feel! What are you going to do about that?

A passion for souls comes out of prayer. And while we don't use prayer simply to help us grow a great church, prayer is foundational to any kind of ministry. You don't have to be known as the most prayerful preacher in the area. You don't have to spend hours and hours in prayer just because some other ministers do, but the effective pastor does need a regular, consistent, substantial prayer life. And that prayer life needs to deal with the task of ministry.

We need to pray about the lost, *O God, what do You expect me to do?* A burden for the lost comes out of prayer.

You can stand on the street corner and watch the masses of people go by, and you may feel some empathy for them, but you'll also feel overwhelmed by the magnitude of trying to reach those people for Christ. It's disheartening to realize how many billions of people are unsaved. The Bible says we're supposed to win the lost, and we try to act on that. But the necessary emotional content will not be there until we get down on our faces before God and grapple with it in prayer, then rise from that place with some kind of conviction that God wants the lost found and the sinful saved, that He is "not willing that any should perish, but that all should come to repentance" (2 Pet. 3:9, KJV) and that He wants you and me to reach them. So we go out with a burning conviction, not just a desire for denominational or personal aggrandizement.

When you reach this point, it doesn't really matter whether or not you have the largest church in town. You just want to reach everyone possible for Christ, and you know in your heart and mind that if you do, the chances are excellent that your church is going to grow. Now, if you're going to reach them, and if you're going to grow, and if you're going to have a wide ministry, your church has to become a different kind of church, but that won't happen just because your motive is right.

We don't pray because we roll out of bed and our knees hit the floor and we think, *While I'm down here, I'll just pray.*

We pray because we have a very definite discipline in our lives. Church growth happens the same way. Your church will grow because you have a very definite discipline for growth. We're so accustomed to spiritualizing things that we think growth is miraculous—that if God wants us to grow, we'll grow, and if He doesn't want us to grow, we're not going to grow. I have yet to meet a person who states, "We're growing, but I just have to be honest with you—we're not doing a thing to cause it." I do meet pastors who admit, "I don't know at this point exactly what it is we're doing that's causing growth," and I meet pastors who acknowledge, as they should, "God is helping us to grow," but I've never met one who said, "We're growing even though I'm not doing anything." They all declare, "I'm working my head off, and several of the people in my church are working like pile drivers too."

When you examine your motives and pray until the drive of your life is to reach the lost, you must follow up with some intentionality. One of the perplexing polarities in life for the Christian is, "How much depends on God, and how much depends on me?" The best anyone has ever been able to resolve that is by suggesting, "Trust as though everything depended on God, and work as though everything depended on you." That has to be incorporated into the plan and the effort to grow. You're doing this because it's essential to the primary task of ministering, and it's the real desire of your heart to reach the lost. Your prayer might be, *And, God, if that's not what I want to do, work on me until that is what I want to do. Work on me until the fundamental motive of my work for growth is to see the lost found, redeemed, and transformed.*

Probably the best way of determining true motivation is by watching action and practice and then evaluating results. Was the action and practice in the direction of bringing recognition to the person? Was the result of the action the advancement of the pastor? Did it result in the salvation of souls? Did, in fact, the church grow, or was it simply a stepping-stone for a minister's career advancement?

The same procedure can also be applied to the pastor who insists that numerical growth is not a noble enough goal. Generally such a person will indicate that it's more important to grow in spiritual depth than it is to grow numerically. Surely no one would question the importance of spiritual growth or of discipleship training in the church, but there's no way to determine the true motive in this kind of commitment. Are the people, in fact, deepening in spiritual things? Is the congregation maturing? Is there a new hunger and thirst for truth and for the Word of God? Is the church growing spiritually, even though it's not growing numerically?

Jesus said, "Ye have not chosen me, but I have chosen you, and ordained you, that ye should go and bring forth fruit, and that your fruit should remain" (John 15:16, KJV). The issue is not activity or inactivity but a question of whether or not the fruit, claimed as the basis for motivation, actually was produced as the *result* of the activity. Only God can determine the driving force of our ministry.

Ideally, a compelling vision from God would be the best motivation for a productive ministry. That was the powerful motivation of Paul's ministry. Jesus appeared to Paul and said,

> I have appeared to you to appoint you as a servant and as a witness of what you have seen of me and what I will show you. I will rescue you from your own people and from the Gentiles. I am sending you to them to open their eyes and turn them from darkness to light, and from the power of Satan to God, so that they may receive forgiveness of sins and a place among those who are sanctified by faith in me (*Acts 26:16-18*).

If only Jesus would appear to us and give us a personalized assignment, we would have a pure motivation. The best we can do is to immerse ourselves in prayer and the Word in quest of special direction from the Lord. Many pastors believe they have received such a vision, and they joyfully follow it, just as Paul was obedient to the heavenly vision.

Lacking such a vision, a pastor may consider the Great Commission as his or her own special assignment from Jesus. "In the past God spoke to our forefathers through the prophets at many times and in various ways, but in these last days he has spoken to us by his Son" (Heb. 1:1-2).

As we examine our motivation for wanting to break through the 200 barrier, we can be confident God wants the lost found, and Jesus has chosen us to make disciples. As a colaborer with Christ in accomplishing God's grand desire, you can lead your church in growth that will result in breaking the 200 barrier.

■ STEP 2 ■
INTENSIFY YOUR PRAYING

One of the remarkable realities of Jesus' life was His dependence upon prayer. His ministry appeared to be based on His prayer life. Repeatedly we're told that Jesus went alone to pray. Before He selected His 12 apostles, He spent the night in prayer (Luke 6:12). Following the miracle of the feeding of the 5,000, Jesus went into the hills alone to pray (Matt. 14:23). Prayer was an important aspect of Jesus' ministry.

Prayer must also be a vital dimension of the pastor's life. He or she can't depend upon training, literary resources, or natural ability alone. The work he or she has been called to do demands far more than human resources can possibly provide. The pastor must have divine help. "Were not the right Man on our side," writes Martin Luther, "our striving would be losing." Without Christ to give us strength in our ministry, we can't hope to succeed in the work He has called us to do. Any hope whatever that we'll be able to build Christ's Church without Christ himself will be completely in vain. Any thought of breaking the 200 barrier and building a great church for the glory of God will be wishful thinking without a vital prayer link with God. It's difficult to explain this, for it does not submit to reason, but it's a reality that has been demonstrated beyond doubt.

It's easy to fall under the accusation that calling for prayer is a utilitarian means of accomplishing a selfish end, but that accusation underestimates the tremendous power of prayer. Prayer changes people. When we pray, we begin to realize our responsibility to be obedient to our Lord. As He asked in His own ministry, "Why do you call me, 'Lord, Lord,' and do not do what I say?" (Luke 6:46). Prayer inevitably brings us to realize that God wants us to reach the lost, to find people who are outside the fold. God wants us to be active in the building of His Church. A strong personal prayer life will effect a transformation of life that will fix our attention on the concerns that move the heart of God.

Personal prayer, however, will not be enough in the long run to build His Church—it will also require corporate prayer. Not every individual member in the church must pray earnestly, but there must be a concerted group effort in prayer that God will help the pastor and church accomplish what He has called them to do. In praying this way, we're seeking not our own desires but rather divine energy to do what He has called us to do, what He has commissioned us to do, what He has charged us to do. We can't do it in our own strength. We must have divine power and intervention. Something happens when God's people get together and pray. It's more than group psychology. Rather, it's His response, "Where two or three come together in my name, there am I with them" (Matt. 18:20). Probably every pastor has observed the phenomenon that when God's people get together and pray, wonderful things happen.

This corporate prayer must be more than occasional and spasmodic. It must be consistent; it must be intense; it must be patient. In a two-day think tank meeting with pastors whose churches had been very effective in evangelism, there was strong agreement that prayer was not only essential but needed to be built into the life of the church. They declared that building space should be given for prayer, that prayer leadership should be staffed with intercessors, and that continual prayer should be scheduled into the program of the church. They were unrelenting in their insistence that prayer was a powerful factor in the growth of the church.

There's something about the time lag between our prayers and the answers that come that tends to weed out those who are not really committed to sincere prayer. Praying requires so much energy and takes so much time before results accrue that those with shallow commitments generally give up before they ever realize any true benefits. So the church that's faithful to its call and obedient to the Lord in moving out to reach the lost and bringing them into the Kingdom must keep on praying until the answer comes.

While it's vitally important that both pastor and people pray, they must also work. Prayer is not a substitute for work—it's the foundation for work. Out of prayer come holy work and holy effectiveness in work. Together they bring dramatic results. As I understand the New Testament, we're asked to pray not until God does the work for us; rather, we're exhorted to pray until God gives us the strength and the power to do the work He has called us to do. So intensify your personal and congregational praying while you move out to work and to win the lost. Break the barrier! Hundreds and hundreds of people will be won to Christ and incorporated into the life of the church.

Jesus declared, "As long as it is day, we must do the work of him who sent me. Night is coming, when no one can work" (John 9:4). There's always a time limit on our opportunities. Realizing that the time is short, we must pray and then get on with the work, never stopping the praying but always working in the power of the Spirit that comes through prayer. This is the only way that praying without ceasing truly makes sense. We continue to pray while we work.

When I took church growth training at Fuller Theological Seminary, I met a young man who was a quick learner and a very articulate spokesman. Six months later, we both returned for a second church growth seminar. At that time we shared some of the things that had been going on in our lives following our initial training. I well remember that this young pastor indicated that he had developed in his church a "PPCG Club." He had all the people talking about it. Only those who agreed to keep the club requirements were allowed to know what the letters stood for: "Please Pray for Church Growth." Today that young man, Kent Hunter, is nationally engaged as a very effective church growth consultant and author of many books. He understood that the very foundation of church growth, or any great work for God, is prayer. If you're to break the 200 barrier in your church, you must intensify your own praying and the praying of your people. Your heart must cry out for them to "please pray for church growth!"

■ STEP 3 ■
INCREASE YOUR FAITH

It's easy to be negative about claims of extraordinary faith. Many overly zealous yet well-intentioned ministers have attempted things for God that they were unable to complete. Although they had announced that they were following unquestionably the leading and will of God, the plan failed and collapsed. Both clergy and laity, observing those experiences, are inclined to speak disdainfully about "mountain-moving faith." Yet it's a biblical concept (1 Cor. 13:2), and it should not be ignored or neglected.

You may respond, "I don't think I have the gift of faith. I'm just not able to believe God for great miracles or to do spectacular things in my ministry." Or you may say, "I would like to have the gift of faith, but I have to be realistic about it. I don't believe I possess it, or if I possess it, it certainly isn't very strong. I need to pray as the disciples asked the Lord, 'Increase our faith!' or as the man who brought his son to Jesus to be healed, 'I do believe; help me overcome my unbelief!'" (Luke 17:5; Mark 9:24).

J. K. Warrick, pastor of College Church of the Nazarene in Olathe, Kansas, spoke to this issue in a sermon on Jesus' words "If you have faith as small as a mustard seed, you can say to this mountain, 'Move from here to there' and it will move. Nothing will be impossible for you" (Matt. 17:20). Dr. Warrick suggested we think of faith as a seed that's inserted into the promises of God. Wherever we need to appropriate one of God's promises, we should simply "drop" the seed of faith into the promise and wait for the seed to sprout, grow, and provide an abundant harvest. We need to overcome our doubt by placing our faith not in our desires but in the promises of God.

A lack of faith results in prayerlessness. This becomes a viscous circle in which a lack of faith hinders us from praying, and prayerlessness deprives us of the power we need for ministry. So increasing our faith is essential to our ministry as well as to effective church growth leadership.

I would like to make six suggestions that, though simple, should help you increase the measure of faith God has given you.

Read about faith in Bible passages like Matt. 21:22, in which Jesus explains the withering of the fig tree; Mark 9:23-24, in which Jesus healed the boy with an evil spirit; Mark 11:24, in which Jesus speaks of asking and believing; Luke 17:5, in which the disciples asked Jesus to increase their faith; Acts 3:16, in which Peter explains how a lame man was healed; Heb. 11:1, in which faith is defined. Read about Abraham, whose life was one great venture of faith. Read about his intervention for his nephew Lot. Read about Moses, who repeatedly moved the heart of God on behalf of the Israelites. Read also about Paul in the New Testament, who moved out in faith to do mighty works for God. You won't have any difficulty finding mountain-moving faith passages. There's power in the Word of God, and you'll be inspired to greater faith.

Read about faith in faith-inspiring books. I would suggest biographies and autobiographies of great people of faith. There are many books about people "who through faith conquered kingdoms, administered justice, and gained what was promised; who shut the mouths of lions, quenched the fury of the flames, and escaped the edge of the sword; whose weakness was turned to strength; and who became powerful in battle and routed foreign armies" (Heb. 11:33-34). Every Christian bookstore has scores of books that recount great accomplishments of faith. Read these books, and your faith will take wings.

Read the stories of great churches. In recent years, many books have appeared on the market telling the story of particular churches and how the faith and vision of their pastors resulted in tremendous ministry. As you read those faith-inspiring books, you'll discover your own faith being strengthened and encouraged.

Look for examples of mountain-moving faith. Watch for people whose lives indicate they have the gift of faith. It may be a fellow minister or a layperson in your church. There should be something about that person's faith that reaps rewards. Watch for it. It will challenge your own faith and encourage you to trust God for great victories. Look for instances in which great vision has resulted in tremendous accomplishment. The Bible says, "Where there is no vision, the people perish" (Prov. 29:18, KJV). There is an implied corollary, "Where there is vision, God's people are built up in their most holy faith," and it's probably accurate to say that the church also grows.

Listen to people of great faith. When you have opportunity to hear persons whom you know to have great faith, listen to them carefully. What do they have to say about faith? How do they describe mountain-moving faith, and what do they recommend to others in regard to increasing their faith? We're all aware that stories of falsification persist against some who claim to be people of faith. True or not, I cannot say. I only recommend that you listen to people you know to be persons of great faith, whose reputations are of good report. Their faith and the victories in their lives will be a great encouragement to your faith.

Ask God to increase your faith as the disciples did, as recorded in Luke 17:5. Jesus' response to the disciples' request is interesting. He didn't say, "All right! That's what I was hoping you'd request." There really isn't much indication He was even delighted. It would seem to us the Lord should have been pleased that the disciples wanted to have more faith, but that was not His response.

On the other hand, He didn't reply, "That's not something you should be asking for." He didn't indicate it was something beyond them or something too sacred for them to concern themselves with. Instead, He replied in essence, "It doesn't take much faith to love and forgive people or to move mountains."

Some of the biblical expositors who deal with this passage relate backward to Jesus' demand that they forgive a brother, even if he or she comes back seven times in the same day requesting forgiveness. Those who look at the passage this way tend to indicate that Jesus is saying, "It isn't *more* faith you need but the *right* kind of faith. And if you have the right kind of faith, you'll indeed be able to forgive your brother."

Other expositors have indicated that faith is like a mustard seed and, though it's very small, it will grow and flourish into a great garden plant, and in time it will develop into a mighty faith that can even move mountains into the midst of the sea.

But whether it's the right kind of faith or a sufficient faith, it's right to pray about it. If Jesus never intended mountain-moving faith to be a part of the Christian's life, then we might wonder why He brought the subject up and why He referred to it on more than one occasion. So don't hesitate to ask God to increase your faith. After all, He has called you to preach the gospel. He has placed you in your present circumstance, and in all likelihood you need mountain-moving faith to accomplish all that He is calling you to do. So pray as the disciples asked the Lord, "Increase our faith!"

Increasing your faith involves acting on your belief. You must not only have faith—you must demonstrate your faith by your works. As leader of the church, not only must you pray that God would work a mighty miracle, but also you must move out in confidence that He will.

Now this is not an exhortation to act on every impression, which might be a zealous but unwise response. It's easy to get excited about mountain-moving faith and attempt something that God hasn't even talked to you about doing. It's easy to get carried away with selfish dreams of grandeur and do something that's not based in the divine will but in the personal ego.

Neither is it a suggestion to disregard wisdom and hazard other people's futures. Many laypersons are skeptical of a pastor's recommendation to move forward in faith because they have previously suffered the consequences of what turned out to be bad judgment rather than genuine faith. This is a delicate area, because some minister might say, "If the people had really trusted God, what we were trying to accomplish would have come to pass." On the other hand, the laypeople might say, "The pastor jumped ship and didn't stay to face the consequences of his [her] action. If his [her] faith had been genuine, he [she] would not have deserted." There's no way to resolve these conflicting perspectives, but they do provide a backdrop against which an appeal for genuine faith may be made. This exhortation to increase your faith is a word of encouragement to seek God's will for your ministry and then simply move out.

It may or may not involve financial risk. Some ministers have increased their credibility in this area by making sure all the financial risk was their own. Generally, we run into trouble when the financial risk we are advocating is someone else's.

Mountain-moving faith will certainly involve risk-taking. You'll probably not accomplish a great work for God until you move into the region of risk. This is the point at which you move out in faith, the place at which you'll discover whether your faith has increased or is still severely lacking. But the probability is great that if you have read about faith, if you've looked for examples of mountain-moving faith, if you've listened to people of great faith, and you've asked God to increase your faith, when you move forward in faith through the power of the Holy Spirit, a great work will be accomplished.

This is not to say that every pastor must have the gift of faith, although a call to the ministry is a call to leadership, and leaders must depend heavily on the gift of faith. The pastors we call church growth pastors tend to have the gift of faith. The probability is that if you went to any large church in North America and became acquainted with the pastor, you would discover that he or she has the gift of faith.

If you don't have the gift of faith, begin praying for God to increase the measure of your faith until you believe in God's ability to work in this world and in His desire to work through you. You must do that in the conviction that God wants you to reach the lost, and that requires building a great church. And because God is going to help you, you *can* build a great church.

A leader who isn't convinced that God wants to build a great church through him or her and reach the lost in great numbers will not be helped by any methodology or opportunity. He or she can be placed in the best growth opportunity in North America, and the church won't grow, because a pastor must believe that God has called him or her to preach the gospel to get people saved, and to enfold them in the church. If the pastor doesn't believe that, no one but the Holy Spirit can help her or him! The most important step in breaking the 200 barrier is to believe that God wants to build a great church through you.

A great church's most important goal is to reach those who are without God, hopelessly and eternally lost. The billions of people who do not know Christ as their Savior, who live in the daily pain of guilt and uncertainty, call for the development and exercise of the gift of faith. If we're going to see growth in our churches, particularly beyond the 200 barrier, we must increase the measure of our faith so we can understand the work God is trying to get done in the world and believe that He wants to do that work through us and in our churches.

6

PLANNING

■ STEP 4 ■
SET A BARRIER-BREAKING GOAL

If you're going to break through the 200 barrier, set a long-range goal that's well beyond the barrier. I suggest the goal be at least 300 and preferably 500. I would not recommend, however, a goal beyond 500. It's a logical numerical point, and if you set the goal beyond 500, it will be perceived as formidable. One of the characteristics of a good goal is that it be realistic. That means it should be possible, with God's help, to achieve the goal. So a realistic goal for breaking through the barrier should be somewhere between 300 and 500. A goal of 300 will be large for a church that's running only 90 to 125, but you'll have several years to achieve it.

Earlier research, based on membership instead of attendance, had indicated that churches tend to break the barrier within three years. That research was done in the earliest years of the personal computer and was based on one 10-year time frame. The present research has been run several times with the aid of current computers and an extensive database. Our conclusions are based on a study of churches that grew from below 150 to above 350 during the 1993—2003 decade. These churches were filtered from a total church count of over 4,000 churches. Only 14 churches matched the criteria. We have run the data for several sets of decades, and it's essentially the same for each decade. For example, during the 1991-2001 decade 17 churches broke the barrier. The original conclusions were based on the 1976-1986 decade, when 29 churches broke the barrier, but that was based on membership instead of attendance.

The "Barrier Breakers '93—'03" graph shows attendance growth of 7 of the 14 churches that broke the barrier during the 1993—2003 decade.

Because so many of the churches are shown on one graph, it's difficult to see a distinctive pattern for a specific church. The "Average and Trend Lines" graph combines all the churches into an average line and a trend line.

When each church is graphed separately, it's possible to see features unique to that particular church. The "Distinctive Growth" graph is for church three in our study. The graph shows the distinctive growth pattern of the church, but its trend line would be similar to the trend line of other churches.

The "Consistent Growth" graph is essentially linear growth. However, it's impressive that this church grew from fewer than 100 to over 500 in 10 years.

From these graphs it's possible to make certain observations:

1. It typically takes 5 years to break the barrier. The average was 5.3 years, and the median was 5 years. Two churches broke the barrier in 3 years, two in 4 years, five in 5 years, one in 6 years, three in 7 years, and one in 8 years.

2. It's not unusual for a church to experience a burst of growth during the decade. This can be seen only on the individual growth graphs. (The "Distinctive Growth" church experienced an increased growth rate during years 8, 9, and 10.) This period of more rapid growth appears to last 3 or 4 years. Of course, this was not the case in churches with linear growth pat-

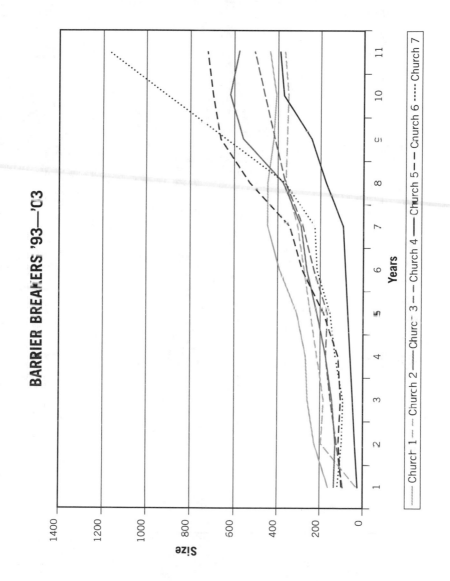

BARRIER BREAKERS '93—'03

Church 1 —— Church 2 —— Church 3 —— Church 4 —— Church 5 —— Church 6 —— Church 7

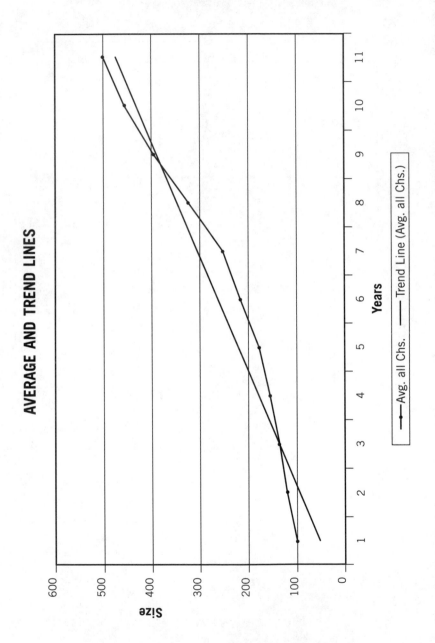

AVERAGE AND TREND LINES

Size

Years

—●— Avg. all Chs.　——— Trend Line (Avg. all Chs.)

DISTINCTIVE GROWTH

CONSISTENT GROWTH

terns. The "Consistent Growth" church never really had a significant increase in growth rate during the decade.

3. Beginning size appears to have no impact on decennial growth. Both the church with the lowest beginning point and the church with the highest beginning point plateaued after breaking the barrier. All the other churches grew to a range of 352 to 1,165. And in the 10th year, 12 of the churches were distributed primarily over a range of 350 to 500.

4. The age of the church was not as significant a factor

as we had assumed. The average number of years the churches have been below 150 in attendance was 15, but since our data reached back only to 1974, the actual average may have been considerably longer. The good news is that your church can break the 200 barrier regardless of its age.

5. Stagnation was not as great a factor as we had anticipated. Ten of the churches were on a plateau or in decline for several years before they began their barrier-breaking growth. Again, the news is good for churches on a plateau or in decline. However, it should be noted that there are contextual factors that limit the possibilities for breaking the barrier.

6. In the large majority of instances, new-convert growth is critical to breaking the barrier. The patterns indicate concerted evangelistic effort rather than consistent biological additions.

7. Transfer growth does not figure significantly in breaking the barrier. This was true in almost every instance, even in rapidly growing suburban areas. Of course, it's possible that some of the new converts should have been listed as transfers in, but the uniformity of the pattern for all churches argues against that possibility.

8. Growth was rapid. Almost two-thirds (64 percent) of the churches grew from below 150 members to over 350 members in 5 years or fewer. Even though the average (based on attendance) is twice the 2.6 years of the 29 churches (based on membership) studied in the original research, it's still a fairly short period of time for a small church to increase 200 in attendance. There is still reason to believe that the best way to break through the 200 barrier is rapidly. There are several reasons why this is true.

Perhaps the best explanation is the power of inspiration and immediate commitment. While tenacity and perseverance are vitally important to church growth, explosive growth seems to come from short periods of inspiration and diligent effort. There's a sense in which the "Pareto principle" is involved here.

Alfred Pareto was an Italian economist who observed that 20 percent of the population possessed 80 percent of the national wealth. Over time, this observation has been widely applied and is now generally understood as indicating that 20 percent of our efforts will produce 80 percent of our results. While this is not normally thought of in terms of time, our research indicates that it may be applicable there as well. Most people are aware they're much more productive on some days than on others. In fact, a careful analysis might reveal that approximately 80 percent of their productive work is accomplished in about 20 percent of their time. While this would undoubtedly be controversial, careful reflection could give some insight into why rapid church growth is the best way to break through the 200 barrier.

The problem with the plan to prepare for growth in the future, to get everything in readiness, to amass the resources, and to design the strategy is that the inspiration cools off before the activity actually begins. To put it bluntly, the plan fizzles out. There just isn't enough strength in a plan. It takes inspiration to make a great plan come to completion. The adage "Do it now" applies to breaking the 200 barrier just as much as to daily discipline.

But there is another reason for planning to break the 200 barrier rapidly. When you try to break the barrier slowly, the social forces that tend to keep an organization small have time to come to bear and prevent it. When people begin to realize they're losing control, that the relationships are changing, and that the style of ministry is changing, they begin to resist it. This may not be at the conscious level. It may be a subconscious response, but the result is the same. When you go through the barrier quickly, people don't have time to discover what's occurring until you're well beyond the barrier.

That sounds devious, but it really isn't. It's simply working with human nature the way it is. When you flood the church with new people and it's growing like gangbusters, the "controllers" and "resisters" rejoice right along with you. If you get beyond the barrier, begin your consolidation, and make the changes necessary to the new organization, you'll already be a different kind of church before there's opportunity to create waves. The church will be large enough in most instances that resistance will be futile. In fact, generally you'll already have a sufficient influx of new people on the board to tilt it toward progress.

We need now to discuss setting a goal that's manageable within existing facilities. "Sociological strangulation" is a church growth term that refers to having run out of space to hold the people. This restriction on growth is real. Space is essential to growth. If you don't have enough, you must build or figure out another way to provide it.

One way to deal with limited capacity is to go to multiple services. However, this must be carefully considered. It can reduce the size of both groups below acceptable levels and be demoralizing to the participants. The dynamic involved is called "critical mass," which is defined as "a size, number, or amount large enough to produce a particular result" *(Merriam-Webster's Dictionary)*. This, of course, varies from church to church and from community to community. There may be other means of dealing with the challenge.

Nursery and toddler children can be kept in their special spaces. Kindergarten, primary, and junior churches are possibilities. Eventually a teen church might be appropriate. There are ways of dealing with sociological strangulation, but you must be creative.

If growing beyond the 200 barrier is impossible in your present facilities, it might be advisable to wait. However, it can be dangerous to wait for adequate facilities, because frequently the motivation to grow is a long time in returning.

■ STEP 5 ■
THINK THROUGH YOUR PLAN

Knowing where you're going is important, but so is knowing how to get there. You know you want to break the 200 barrier by growing, but what will produce growth, and what changes and resources will be needed in the process? It isn't necessary to plan in detail everything that's going to happen over the next several years, but it's very important to have thought through what's going to take place as the church grows through the 200 barrier. The barrier is such a formidable obstacle to continued growth that the only hope of breaking through it is to be knowledgeable and prepared to overcome it in the most effective and efficient way possible. A cavalier approach is almost certain to fail.

Perhaps the first task is to *think through the growth principles* on which strategies for breaking the barrier can be developed.

The first and most important consideration is the spiritual. God wants the church to grow. Christ has commissioned His followers to "make disciples" throughout the world. You have a divine call to "preach the gospel" or, at least, an assigned responsibility. The Holy Spirit indwells individual believers to empower them for life, service, and witness. God's prevenient grace comes to people before they come to Him. There really appears to be no doubt that your assignment is to lead the church in growth. You're not waiting on directions from God. He's waiting on your obedience to His already-revealed will. So obedience is your part in the divine-human cooperative. But how will you go about accomplishing God's call on your life?

Most Christians work in harmony with concepts that seem to make sense. They either follow traditional methods, or they try new ones that appear effective. In both instances, Christians have used their mind to determine their actions. The Book of Proverbs in the Old Testament is basically a collection of observations on how life works. Today we have a collection of observations on how the church most effectively wins and disciples people into faith in Christ. It takes note of *contextual factors* such as demographics and *institutional factors* such as the culture of a congregation. Taking these factors into consideration in planning to break the 200 barrier is using your mind to increase your effectiveness in obeying Christ's commission. There are many social and psychological insights that are useful in leading the church in growth. For example, C. Peter Wagner lists five institutional factors that tend to keep a church under the 200 barrier.

1. The desire to preserve social intimacy.
2. The desire to maintain control.
3. The desire to conserve memories.
4. The desire to protect turf.
5. The desire to remain comfortable.[1]

Wagner also lists some contextual factors that impact growth. He describes the challenge that arises when the community surrounding the church changes to a profile that's different from the people in the church. He also explains the negative impact on a church when the community population severely declines.

Understanding the impact of these factors and other sociological factors can greatly aid in accomplishing what you believe is God's will for your life. Just as you would not hesitate to use the tools of technology in evangelism, take advantage of the insights of sociology to develop the most effective methods of evangelism. And learn from the literature on leadership, just as Moses learned from his father-in-law, Jethro, how to manage and lead the people of Israel.

Leadership is a significant human factor in guiding and developing the church. A *position* of leadership is not adequate. A leader whom people actually follow is necessary for the advance of the church. A leader must have faith and the ability to communicate it. John Maxwell explains, "Good leaders possess faith—great leaders communicate faith."[2] Faith leads to a vision of what God wants done and to confidence in setting goals that can be achieved in the power of the Holy Spirit.

Strong leadership requires a commitment that runs contrary to widespread assumptions about the ministry. George Hunter points out that Richard Baxter's book *The Reformed Pastor,* first published in 1656, has probably shaped Protestant assumptions on the job description of a pastor more than any other 10 books combined. Baxter, a Puritan pastor in an English town of 800 homes, "served as every person's evangelist, catechist, teacher, and preacher (Sunday morning and evening); he took it on himself to minister to all sick people and to visit from house to house."[3]

A growth leader understands that as numbers increase, such a job description is not only impossible but actually flawed in its fundamental premise. It professionalizes ministry, which in reality belongs to all believers. The Christian leader's responsibility is not to do all the ministry that really matters but to make sure the ministry of the church is properly focused and directed.

Lyle Schaller, in contrast to Baxter, explained (as stated earlier) that as a church grows larger, the pastoral role must change from that of "shepherd" to "rancher." Instead of providing all the "shepherding" care to one flock, the pastor must provide the "ranching" oversight to multiple flocks. Carl George has provided greater detail of this concept by listing the five behaviors of each pastoral role.

Behaviors of shepherds:
1. Personally provide all the caring
2. Attempt to meet all the expectations
3. Work to the limit of abilities
4. Keep work close to them
5. Allow perspectives to be dominated by the present

Behaviors of ranchers:
1. Concerned for high-quality pastoral care
2. Set expectations
3. Perceive the church organizationally rather than personally
4. Delegate and involve others
5. Develop management skills[4]

The shepherd/rancher differentiation has become widely accepted as a model of ministry. Many pastors are attempting to serve their small church as a rancher, misunderstanding that the rancher role is for large churches. As one observer noted, "You can't be a rancher if you don't have a ranch." However, one theory of church growth suggests that a small church should think like a large church. That's probably the reason pastors of small churches adopt the rancher role.

In the adoption of the rancher role, it's still imperative that the work of ministry gets done. Some pastors take the position that ministry is the role of the laity and that if it doesn't get done, it's their fault. That, of course, is true, but it's a fatal mistake to forget where the buck stops! The task of the pastor is not merely to inform the laity that ministry is their responsibility but also to inspire the laity to do the work. If the pastor is unable to motivate the laity to perform the ministry, he or she probably does not have the capability to be a rancher. He or she will have to learn how to be a rancher or find a flock he or she can shepherd.

A pastor seeking to break the 200 barrier will also need to think through the strategies that are available for use. Wagner explains, "Strategy is the chosen means to accomplish a pre-determined goal."[5] Since there are many growth-producing methods and programs, it's important to think through the possibilities and choose the one or ones that best fit your situation. It would require excessive space to list all of the growth methods available, much less evaluate them. Instead, I'll explain two major overall strategies that may be applied in a variety of ways. The first is *lay mobilization.*

We've already suggested that ministry is the task of each and every believer. Unfortunately, in our culture that conviction is not widely shared among the laity. Centuries of control by professional ministers has almost completely clouded the biblical example of laity in ministry. This is true even though from time to time there have been attempts to restore the laity to their rightful role. And it's still a widespread assumption even though observation is convincing that the laity is much more effective in ministry than the clergy.

The wise biblical strategist will work to mobilize the laity in ministry and evangelism. John Maxwell lists seven ways to motivate people into ministry:

1. Believe in your people. They are your only appreciable asset.
2. Develop a process for commitment to ministry. You must have a system that discovers people's spiritual gifts and matches them for ministry assignments.

3. Model your priorities. People do what people see.
4. Highlight those who are doing the ministry. Make heroes out of lay ministers. Make everyone's ministry important.
5. Develop an outreach ministry that involves everyone.
6. Set goals that will encourage and expand the people.
7. Remove the fear of failure. What would you do for God if you knew you would not fail?[6]

Almost any program that's built on utilizing the gifts and abilities of the laity in ministry will be more effective than programs that do not.

Another major strategy for growth is organizational in nature. It builds on the fact that as organizational units multiply, more individuals come into the organization. Elsewhere, we discuss the multiplication of groups as a growth thrust. Again, almost any program that significantly increases the number of groups will produce numerical growth in the congregation.

Along with the multiplication of organizational units, the change in organizational operation will significantly facilitate growth. Five organizational developments give indication of the enormity of change that occurs in breaking the 200 barrier:

1. *From association to organization.* A small church is an association of people sharing a common concern. If the small congregation grows through the 200 barrier, it will lose its associational relationship and become an organization with structures, positions, and policies.

2. *From single-cell to multiple groups.* A small church is a single cell of people in relationship. If the small church grows through the 200 barrier, it will become an organization of multiple cells. This will be a complete change in the extent of relationships between the people and between the pastor and the people.

3. *From shepherd to rancher.* When a small church grows through the 200 barrier, the pastor will no longer be able to have a personal relationship with all the people in the congregation. The pastor will have to become the leader of the organization and depend on others to provide the pastoral care for the people.

4. *From one pastor to multiple staff.* A small church that grows through the 200 barrier will need additional staff to provide specialized leadership for ministry assignments and training for lay leaders.

5. *From board-led to staff-led.* When a small church grows through the 200 barrier, the multiplicity of programs and large number of constituents will require operational decisions that can't wait for a church board to convene. Increasingly, major operational decisions will be made by the staff, and the board will take on an advisory role.

Early in the process, the pastor should think through the principles and strategies for breaking the 200 barrier. The thinking will not be complete, however, until the pastor has *thought through the implementation* for breaking the 200 barrier.

How are you going to launch the project? How will you answer your critics? (You *will* have critics.) How will you finance the project? (It's going to cost money.) What are you going to do when you break the barrier? Do you have the physical and emotional energy to keep the project going? Is this something you're going to do for only a year or two and then back off and catch your breath? Even though it's a matter of commitment, such a project requires that you be certain you have the physical and emotional energy to carry it to completion.

Some pastors have had growth as their goal, but when growth came, they discovered they had overextended themselves. They had neither the pastoral staff nor the lay leaders to do what needed to be done. They ran into an impossible situation so far as facilities were concerned, and they didn't know how to resolve it. They hadn't even thought about it!

You can't have all the answers—you don't know what the questions are. But you can think through your plan and say, "Now, here's what I think I'll do when a certain situation arises. If that doesn't work, I'll be ready for the situation and do something else about it."

Don't over-plan. It takes too long, it consumes too much energy that can be used for growth, and it will have to be altered from time to time anyway. A plan is something you're going to do if you don't do something else. Sound foolish? It isn't. Circumstances change no matter how you plan. Nine times out of ten, the major aspects of your plan will work; but if something comes along that's more important or more significant, change your plan or modify it. The probabilities are that if you plan in great detail, much of the detail is going to be scrapped because you're going to discover it didn't fit what actually happened. It's sufficient to set your direction and think through your plan of action.

What's really crucial is communication. It's without doubt the number-one failing of most leaders. The communication process is so complex and fraught with "glitches" that it's amazing that even 10 percent of communication is actually successful. Yet pastors continue leading headlong toward almost impossible challenges, assuming their followers are fully informed about the task and how to accomplish it! It's no wonder congregations don't follow. They haven't the slightest idea what's going on! But leaders will insist that they've fully informed their people.

I'm reminded of a lady who told me her grandmother used to ask her husband to do a certain task. Later, when she asked him if he had completed the task, he would declare that his wife never had asked him. The wife would insist that she had told him, and he would insist that she had not told him. When in exasperation she declared one last time that she had indeed told him, he would reply, "Well, you might have told me, but you didn't *get* me told!" That's the problem with communication between most pastors and their congregations. More heartache springs from poor communication than from a busload of problem people! Unless a pastor can get his or her people to understand and "buy in" to the vision and goals of the strategy, there's little hope for successful implementation.

Securing volunteers to help with the task will be a critical challenge. If you plan to break the 200 barrier, you are going to take the church to a size of operation it has never before experienced. It will necessitate a higher level of competency in workers than previously required. So recruitment will be critical. If you staff with enthused but minimally competent people, you'll be headed for anxiety. Gene Grate, who publishes Real Life Resources on Compact Discs, has developed a helpful chart for understanding factors involved in "Leading Your Church Through Change."[7] The chart on the following page shows five factors involved in securing change and the result if one of the factors is missing.

If the recruits possess the necessary skills but lack incentive, the best you can hope for is gradual change and slow, or no, growth. Look for ability and motivation in securing volunteers to help break the 200 barrier.

Finally, think through how you'll resource growth and expansion as your implementation unfolds. The most obvious resource needed will be money. Often when a pastor projects the financial needs for growth, he or she greatly underestimates the cost of dramatically increased overhead. The heat-

LEADING YOUR CHURCH THROUGH CHANGE

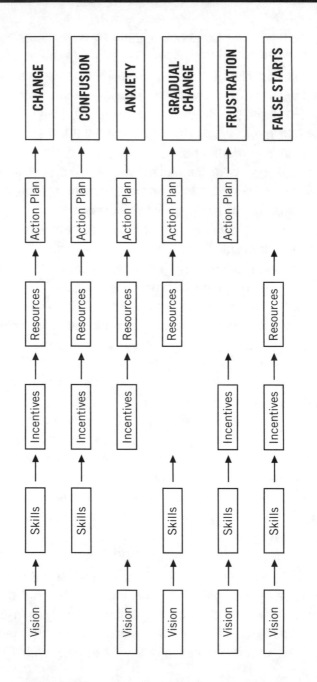

Vision	Skills	Incentives	Resources	Action Plan	=	CHANGE
Vision	Skills	Incentives	Resources	Action Plan	=	CONFUSION
Vision	Skills		Resources	Action Plan	=	ANXIETY
Vision	Skills	Incentives	Resources	Action Plan	=	GRADUAL CHANGE
Vision	Skills	Incentives		Action Plan	=	FRUSTRATION
Vision	Skills	Incentives	Resources		=	FALSE STARTS

ing bill may not increase, but janitorial expenses may escalate with the added traffic.

To take care of the increasing numbers, new and updated equipment will be required. Technological advances have provided much greater efficiency for church offices, but the price tag is not cheap. With the equipment comes the necessity for increased supplies.

And if all this isn't enough, program costs go up dramatically. It's difficult to run a growing church on the same program expenditures that were available for a smaller church.

The need for remodeling certain areas of the building as a result of growth is bound to come. Frequently enlargements to the physical plant must be made, and increased parking space is required. The lot next door that the church hoped someday to purchase will have to be bought sooner than anticipated. Not that the significantly greater cost of operating a larger church isn't worth it, but pastors frequently underestimate the cost.

When I was pastoring a smaller church, I used to look at the larger churches and wonder what they did with all their money. I thought if we just had that much income, we could do remarkable things, yet the realities are that most larger churches struggle to maintain their commitments. What is usually not understood is there are no economies of scale in service organizations. It actually costs more for a large church to operate per member than for a small church.

Money is one of the areas in which the church board becomes very much involved, and conflicts occur over the necessity of certain expenditures. Managing growth means managing the expanding finances. It means thinking ahead to what your priorities are going to be for expenditures within a given year. It means anticipating the new program items you're going to add to the schedule and planning how you're going to finance them. It means demonstrating to your church board and to your people that you know how to allocate the funds of the church so that programs can grow and expand without taking the church into insolvency. This is why it's so vitally important for the pastor to think through his or her resource needs.

The second resource area is facilities. Projections for housing worship, administration, education, and fellowship activities are generally inadequate. It isn't easy to know how much space will be required for growth. Parking also becomes a problem. Additional land is very expensive if it's available at all. In many instances there simply are no possibilities for expansion. The only alternative is to contemplate a move or start a new church. However, starting a new church usually generates missional enthusiasm and results in the growth of the sponsor church.

When a move is undertaken, not only is there tradition and emotional attachment—there's also the reordering of priorities and target groups for the church. The need for facilities to house growth presses the pastor who would lead his or her people into expansion to think through his or her resource needs. What will growth in this locale mean and require? Do we have the emotional energy and the commitment to see it through?

The third resource that pastors tend to overlook or underestimate concerns staff. I'm coming increasingly to believe that the reason many churches are not growing larger is that they're not developing a sufficient staff quickly enough. They may get one staff member and think they're very progressive when, in fact, they really should have hired two. Despite the economic factors, to move a church into the 300-to-500 category, staff must be expanded soon enough and large enough.

If the increased staff is properly deployed and supervised, they'll pay for themselves. At the time of hiring, you probably need only half the necessary annual money.

I always expected a staff person to pull about 10 couples around himself or herself, 2 or 3 of these being families already in the church. It's only logical that some people in the church are going to relate to the new staff member and become their right-hand workers. That's fine. But beyond those I expected them to pull about 6 or 7 other couples out of our prospect list. When they do that and get them saved and contributing to the church, they're going to pay for themselves.

It needs to be plainly stated here that we're not talking about multiplying staff as an ecclesiastical status symbol. Not at all! Some pastors think they have it made when they can hire a full-time staff person. This does not make a church a large church. And we're certainly not talking about creating staff so that the pastor doesn't have to work as hard. As every senior pastor knows, each staff person added means working harder. You really have to keep ahead of your staff to effectively utilize them. We're talking about making it harder on the pastor, but we're ultimately talking about expanding the opportunity for the church to grow.

Staff persons should not be considered as assistant ministers who do the same things as the senior pastor at a different level, or persons to whom the leader can delegate the things he or she really didn't want to do. That's the wrong philosophy, of course. The staff person should be an extension of the ministry, making it possible to accomplish more in special areas, such as youth, music, and evangelization.

When you hire staff, volunteer people tend to say, "Thank the Lord—we finally have someone paid to do that task. Now I don't have to do it." That's a misinterpretation of reality, though it's a typical response of people who have worked in small churches all their lives. They haven't matured in their organizational perspective to the point that they understand staff people are not hired to do their work but to train them to work more effectively to reach more people and offer more services and ministries. If you don't get a staff person who understands that, you're going to have to train that person in a hurry. Generally, it's up to you to train your staff to understand what their task is, and it's very important that they in turn not allow people to back off from volunteer responsibilities.

The attitude of "We're not going to hire someone until we absolutely have to" is also self-defeating, though I once believed and accepted that philosophy. A church needs rather to ask, "What is it that needs to be done?" and "Are we at the point that someway, somehow we can hire a staff person who will enable us to move out in dramatic and effective ways of ministry?" That's a perspective I believe is workable. The smaller church of necessity may need to begin by hiring a part-time secretary and/or a part-time music director, or even using volunteers. Later these may become full-time staff persons on a paid basis. Some laypeople really want to keep from proliferating staff, to keep the organization as small as possible. Such a nonproductive attitude needs to be overcome. Growth comes only through aggressive action and activity.

There's a distinct difference between a staff-run church and a staff-*led* church. Staff persons who fail to develop lay leaders in their respective positions are making a serious mistake. It's not possible to hire enough staff to generate and operate a highly developed church program and ministry. Only through the involvement and development of laypersons can a church hope to expand its ministry and become a great church.

Another resource need the pastor will have to consider is his or her own energy and commitment. There will be an excessive demand on the pastor for personal commitment, energy, and persistence. Leading a church in growth is not easy. It will not permit laziness nor allow an inordinate amount of recreation. In fact, it will probably be more demanding than it should be, requiring commitments that ordinarily would not be made. It will require rising early and working late as a regular schedule. Responding to impossible demands for ministry will require enormous amounts of energy, far more than the pastor anticipated when he or she began to lead the growth thrust. It may be tolerable the first year or the second year, and maybe even the third or fourth, but ultimately it will take its toll.

Unfortunately, the pastor cannot opt to simply walk away. A dream is involved. A vision is involved. More people than the pastor are committed to this dream and vision. The pastor can't desert the people who believed him or her when he or she articulated the dream and declared that he or she was willing to pay the price if they would follow him or her. The pastor must find a way to preserve his or her health, to save his or her family, and to save his or her own soul and still persevere in pursuit of the dream and the vision God gave him or her on the mountain, to which his or her people so joyfully and faithfully responded. Such a pastor will stick with it when the demands become unreasonable.

When the pastor determines that he or she is going to lead the church to 300, 500, or beyond, he or she must anticipate the resource needs and plan how he or she is going to meet them, respond to them, and overcome them. Thinking through the resource needs is one of the most important steps in breaking the 200 barrier.

■ STEP 6 ■
FOCUS ON THE CRITICAL FEW

Knowing what produces growth in a particular situation is difficult. There are many variables. Cities, towns, and communities have characteristics unique to their location, population, economy, and history. Within those settings, local churches have their own congregational culture that's based on community culture but is modified with beliefs, practices, people, and organizational history. While there's considerable similarity among congregations based on human nature and national characteristics—such as economy, education, communication, and general values—it's difficult to design a growth strategy that will work in most churches. Local church leaders continue to learn that growth strategies must be adapted and tailored for their particular situation.

Not only must growth strategies be adapted for local situations—they must also be examined for true growth-producing practices. There are many good and worthwhile ministries for churches to embrace. At certain times in the life of the church those ministries may be highly appropriate and beneficial to the church and community. But if a congregation desires to grow in such a way as to break the 200 barrier, they must make certain their strategies are truly growth-producing.

One of the most important aspects of breaking through the 200 barrier is to concentrate your energies on only two or three activities. This recommendation follows the reasoning of the management principle called the "critical few." Louis A. Allen's *Professional Manager's Guide* defines the critical few as follows: "In any given group of occurrences, a small number of causes will tend to give rise to the largest proportion of results."[8]

Focusing on the critical few is recommended as one of the steps, not because it's a management principle, but because its effectiveness is easily observed in practice. This is particularly true in rapid growth. It may be a little more difficult to explain slow growth, but rapid growth can generally be accounted for by one or two factors of the church. Of course, the question is "Which few activities should I concentrate on?"

The answer is both simple and difficult. I'll list three fairly obvious essentials to growth and proceed to explain how to accomplish them even though they're difficult to achieve.

Openness to change is necessary for a congregation to grow into a larger-size church. Getting people to change is more than an individual assignment. It's a group task. The culture of the congregation must be directed into new values and practices. It's commonly understood that small churches value face-to-face relationships. The people in small churches will react and respond to factors necessary for growth in keeping with their high priority on face-to-face relationships. In most instances their responses will be counterproductive to growth. Interestingly, such congregational responses may often be at the subconscious level. People will insist they want the church to grow and may even criticize the pastor for inadequate growth leadership. Yet even while they're affirming support for growth, they'll be making subconscious decisions that prevent growth. Dealing with this phenomenon is sensitive and complicated.

The second essential for growth among the critical few factors is *visitors*. This is such an obvious and simple requirement that its true importance is often overlooked. Visitors are the necessary input for the output of growth.

In compliance with an organizational seminar I attended a few years ago, I read a book by Ram Charan titled *What the CEO Wants You to Know*. The thesis is that there are five things every business has in common regardless of size. These five things are essential to street vendors and also to large multinational corporations: cash flow, margin, velocity, growth, and customers.[9]

It was so fundamental and fascinating that it caused me to wonder if there are comparable specific essential factors in the growth of the church. Is it possible there are certain factors that are as essential for a megachurch as they are for a very small church?

I've been working on that possibility and testing it on several pastors. I have developed a list of five essential factors. But before I share them with you, I want to offer some disclaimers.

First, these factors are all about numerical growth. They assume prayer, faith, love, and all those glorious characteristics that make the Christian Church the kingdom of God among us. Some pastors may want to stop reading right now, for you say you don't care about numerical growth. Well, let me tell you what I think about that with just five words I've borrowed from some of George G. Hunter's humorous expressions: Horsefeathers! Baloney! Hogwash! Poppycock! Balderdash! Of course you care about growth. Anyone who cares about the kingdom of God cares about the growth of the church. I have yet to meet a preacher who would rather preach to an empty church than to a full one. If you think you don't care about the numerical growth of your church—think again!

Second, these universal factors don't do away with the need for Christian community and nurture. There are still many aspects of church life that are essential to the well-being of the church. So I would say that while these factors are necessary, even essential, they're not everything. You must have them, but you must have more.

Third, these factors are not profound. In fact, they're so simple that you'll wonder how I have the courage to even mention them in print.

So with those disclaimers, let me share with you my five essential factors, based on Ram Charan's model, in the growth of any church regardless of size:

1. *Visitors (cash flow).* How do you get visitors?
2. *Return visitors (margin).* What makes visitors return?
3. *Converts (velocity).* What causes visitors to accept the values and beliefs of the church?
4. *Organizational development (growth).* What structures are necessary to contain and facilitate continued growth?
5. *Attendees who recommend the church (customers).* How do you generate enthusiasm about the church?

I told you they weren't profound—but don't dismiss them too quickly. You would be hard-pressed to disprove them, and if a church is on a growth plateau, or in decline, I'm relatively sure they're not doing as well as they could and should in these areas.

The U.S. Congregational Life Survey[10] discovered that two percent of the attendees in a typical morning worship service are first-time visitors. Keep in mind that a person can be a first-time visitor only once at a specific church. This means that a typical church of 100 will probably have around 100 first-time visitors per year. Since most churches are on a growth plateau, it's possible to infer that more than two percent first-time visitors are required in order to grow.

First-time visitors are unquestionably one of "the critical few" factors to congregational growth. Serious consideration and energetic action should be given to increasing the number of these visitors to the programs and services of the church.

As important as first-time visitors are to growth, return visitors are even more important. A return visitor is a much better prospect than a first-time visitor, and a visitor who returns a third and fourth time is an infinitely greater prospect.

Returning for second, third and fourth visits indicates that the visitor has found something attractive and promising in the church. It's vital for a church to be the kind of church to which first-time visitors will want to return.

Good-quality worship services are the third item in the critical few factors of congregational growth. Good-quality programming requires more than resources. Attitude and planning are essential components of good-quality programming. If a leader thinks that because a congregation is small, good-quality programming is not important, then less-than-good-quality programming will surely result. If, on the other hand, the leader strives to provide the highest quality of programming with available resources, the church will discover that they're not as resource-deficient as they might have assumed. Planning can provide variety, interest, surprise, excitement, discovery, and several other resources for good-quality programming. Musical talent is not the only resource for good-quality programming in the small church. In fact, the informal nature of the small church favors resources other than performance talents.

A word needs to be said about the informality of small congregations. The informal, casual, personal, and spontaneous nature of small congregational gatherings is both an asset and a liability. The asset is obvious. The liability must be delicately managed. The casualness is intertwined with the culture of the people. An attempt to diminish the casualness may be perceived as contrary to "the way we are." Planning good-quality services should build on the casual culture. The planning can bring to the congregational culture new and exciting dimensions of worship and fellowship.

Thought should also be given to the way visitors from the community perceive the informality of the worship services. First-time visitors may feel very awkward in informal settings with people they don't know. These feelings will be increased if many of the people in the congregation don't appear friendly. It's the responsibility of the congregation to "break the ice," and if they don't, as is usually the case, the visitor feels extremely uneasy in the setting and will probably not return. Of course, planning and programming don't eliminate this situation, but they can alter the setting in such a way as to reduce the tension for visitors. Strict adherence to starting time and ending at a reasonable time are important to most people in time-conscious North America. Appropriate leadership and obvious direction provide a sense of unity and purpose to the service. A personal and informal introduction of a planned service element can preserve the casual spirit without conveying a haphazard, nobody-knows-what's-going-on situation. A well-thought-out sermon with everyday help for contemporary people will always be appropriate for any worship service—and will be a powerful factor in causing visitors to return.

Congregations need to be trained to appreciate worship services that appeal to visitors. That doesn't mean they will no longer be ministered to themselves. But it does mean services and ministries will no longer be focused exclusively on the members or provided solely for their benefit.

So many people think church services are boring. Multiplied thousands refuse to attend. Unfortunately, thoughtless approaches to planning and leading worship services proves them right!

(1) Openness to change, (2) visitors, and (3) good-quality worship services are the three "critical few" factors I would recommend in attempting to break the 200 barrier. Careful attention should be given to how your church will focus on the critical few.

7
IMPLEMENTING

■ STEP 7 ■
CREATE EXCITEMENT

Create excitement. "Sure!" you might say. "Abracadabra! What other miracle do you want me to perform?" Well, I admit that excitement is difficult to produce, but it's an important factor in getting a church growing and in sustaining growth. Some people seem to create excitement without trying. Others work with great intentionality to accomplish it. Here are 10 possible ways excitement can be created.

1. *Pray.* A wellspring of joy, love, faith, and expectation will emerge as you pray. Pray that God will bring a great sense of excitement and victory to your life and to the lives of your people that will spill over into the public services.

2. *Promote and express positive thinking.* This sparks anticipation, it supports joy, and it overcomes trouble. We're not talking about spiritual hype but about developing a positive mental attitude. Even if positive thinking is considered secular or humanistic, it works. If you think you can, you're right. If you think you can't, you're still right.

The most profound concept I learned from the positive-thinking advocates is that the mind is like a field. It will grow anything you plant in it. If you plant weeds in a field, it'll grow weeds. If you plant corn, it'll grow corn. If you plant cotton, it'll grow cotton. The same is true of the mind. If you sow negative thoughts, you'll reap negative thoughts. If you sow positive thoughts, you'll reap the same.

I once did not believe this, but I've struggled with some thought processes that were the result of conditioning I allowed years ago when I didn't think it mattered. I didn't believe those who said, "Sow a thought and reap a desire." Now, every time I intentionally, forcefully, and deliberately force out the negative thinking I allowed and make myself think positively, I reap a wonderful harvest.

Helping people think positively is one of your pastoral tasks. Ask and you will receive; seek and you will find; knock and it will be opened to you (see Matt. 7:7-8; Luke 11:9-10). These do not necessarily indicate health, wealth, and fame, but they point toward a balanced approach to life. Neither do they suggest refusing to admit that there is sorrow, heartache, sin, disease, and pain in the world. Rather, it means recognizing those problems, believing that God will enable us to rise above them. Happiness in life is largely a matter of attitude. Millionaires are often miserable, while others who have barely enough to buy groceries are radiantly happy. Positive thinking is essential to creating excitement, and when pastors stand in the pulpit, they must be positive.

In my first pastorate, information was sometimes funneled to me that indicated I wasn't feeding the people. That made no sense to me, because I knew I was preaching the gospel. I was into Paul like you wouldn't believe, and I thought I was doing a good job! What were my critics talking about? In my second pastorate, I remember sitting in my office one day and questioning myself, *Will this sermon help anyone? Will it encourage anyone? Will it lift someone up?* I began building sermons that way and discovered immediately the difference it made. During my first pastorate I had said in effect to the people, "You brood of vipers! Who warned you to flee from the coming wrath?" (Matt. 3:7; Luke 3:7). I didn't realize how negatively based it was. Figuratively, people came crawling into church. They had been beaten down by the world and were almost ready to give up. They struggled to be in church, and they looked at me as if to say, *Preacher, do you have a good word for me today? Does God have anything to say to me about this mess I'm living in?*

In my second pastorate I preached texts like "My grace is sufficient for you, for my power is made perfect in weakness" (2 Cor. 12:9). Some may say I compromised—stopped preaching the whole gospel. No, I still preached on hell, on the lost condition of humanity, on judgment. I still preached on commitment and self-denial, but not all the time. And every Sunday I asked myself those same questions to test the helpfulness of my sermons. I actually practiced making helpful statements, though at first it sounded phony to me. I was so used to admonishing people to be better and work harder for the Lord. I began saying to them, "Hey, it's wonderful to serve God. He knows all about your situation, and He'll give you the strength to face it." That's what I mean by radiating from the pulpit. Accentuate the positive.

3. *Encourage enthusiasm.* It lifts people's spirits. It's catching. Be genuine, but be enthusiastic. I learned from Curtis Smith that when you're going to the pulpit, you should get there in a hurry and act as though it's worth being there. I see pastors saunter to the pulpit as if they dreaded it. If you're going to create excitement, you must be enthusiastic and speak with enthusiasm.

"Well, that's not me," you may say. Then be as enthusiastic as you can. Obviously some people are so enthusiastic that they bounce off the wall. You don't have to be like them, but you can be positive and speak with as much enthusiasm as you can possibly generate.

My first experience with a megachurch was in 1957 with Calvary Temple, an independent congregation in Denver. At that time, only two churches in my denomination had more than 1,000 members, and there probably weren't 50 megachurches in any denomination in North America. When I asked about the secret of Calvary Temple's growth, I was told that it was the enthusiasm of the people.

- They were excited about their church.
- They recommended it to their friends.

That was over 46 years ago, when the church growth movement was only two years old. Donald McGavran's book *The Bridges of God*, which launched the movement, had just been published and was the only book on the subject. Now, over four decades and hundreds of books later, one of the best explanations for outstanding church growth is still the enthusiasm of people about their church.

Some people consider enthusiasm a worldly and insincere emotion. Actually, the opposite is true. The two Greek words used for "enthusiasm" mean "God inside you." What better source of enthusiasm is there than God inside you?

Phineas F. Bresee declared, "If any man loses his enthusiasm, he might as well be buried." He knew that a lack of enthusiasm "is one of the greatest hindrances to the work of God." He even said a lack of enthusiasm "is sure evidence that the heavenly vision is dim."

The truth is that enthusiasm is simply faith in action. It is the logical expression of the joyful knowledge of God's good news for the world.

Ralph Waldo Emerson insisted that "every great and commanding movement in the annals of the world is the triumph of enthusiasm. Nothing great was ever achieved without it."

Every large church is the triumph of the enthusiasm of its people.

4. *Set realistic goals.* Make them challenging but possible. A good goal will require special effort and divine help, but if it's impossible, it will discourage people instead of excite them. A goal gives people something to get excited about. Most people want to attempt the extraordinary, and they get excited about the possibilities of achieving it.

5. *Spiritualize the work of the church in your communication to people.* In your promotion from the pulpit and in newsletters, communicate to your people that seeing souls saved and rebuilding lives is what the work of the church is all about. You're not just increasing numbers or erecting buildings—you're doing God's work. Read the newsletters of exciting churches, and you'll discover that everything is spiritually oriented. They don't just raise money. They ask their people to make a great gift to God. They aren't merely constructing a building—they're providing a place for people who are going to be won as a result of faithful stewardship. They could say, "You owe 10 percent of your income to the Lord, and you ought to give another 5 percent to help us do some of the things we're trying to do as a church," and people would say, "We can't do it. We have too many personal bills." But if you say to them, "We're doing a great work for God, and you have a chance to share in this tremendous ministry—you can make an investment in the kingdom of God," then they'll do it. Learn the secret of spiritualizing the work of the church. Is that honest? Yes, it is. The Bible says to do everything you do to the glory of God.

6. *Celebrate victories and successes.* This is extremely important. Every time someone gets saved, give it special attention in the public services. Every time someone has an answer to prayer that's significant, report it in a public service and in the newsletter. Help the people feel something's happening at their church, that something wonderful is going on all the time.

7. *Focus on people's needs and help them.* I venture to say that most of those attending your church would be impressed if they knew the church was actually helping people, whether it was by providing meals, giving them clothes, or helping them through problems. This is where love, acceptance, and forgiveness are important. You don't have to condone their problems or their sins, but you do need to love people. You do need to accept them just as they are, and you do need to forgive them for their wrongdoing. When you focus on people's needs, you'll discover that even the folk who never want the church to do anything except preach the gospel will be impressed that their church is really helping people.

8. *Plan outstanding programs.* We have the makings of boredom in our churches. The makings of monotony and boredom are there because we have 52 Sunday morning services when we do about the same things with the same people. That can get boring. So plan some outstanding programs.

Plan a musical, or something that's really big and new that challenges the folk to get other people involved in doing something different. We used to create excitement in my church by adding variety. People would say our church services were never the same twice. Not everyone can handle variety, but do something to give the people a feeling of expectancy.

9. *Develop inspiring worship services.* There's considerable variety in what inspires people. Some are moved by quiet meditation; others prefer emotional expression. Symbolism and pageantry inspire some, while others are moved only by great thoughts—especially biblical truths. Today many prefer contemporary Christian music, while many older attendees prefer hymns and organ music.

Planning an inspiring worship service with the great variety of preferences is admittedly difficult. On the one hand, if you try to have something for everyone, you may not satisfy anyone.

On the other hand, if you specialize on too narrow of a segment of the population, you may reach only a few people.

I would suggest two concepts to keep in mind as you try to involve the people in your community in worship. (1) Remember—you build a church on young families. The future always belongs to the younger generation. Evangelism is primarily a youth activity. (2) "Contemporary" is more than music. "Contemporary" is a mind-set and is more about how the sermon is crafted and presented than it is about drums, guitars, and casual dress. I have a growing feeling that we've tried to model our churches after great contemporary churches and have picked up their form instead of their essence. We need to capture their essence as well as their form, because form without essence is meaningless.

Someway, somehow learn to connect with the people who will be attending your worship services, and provide for them great moments of inspiration.

10. *Secure renowned guest speakers and singers from time to time.* You may need to grow before you can incorporate them into your program in significant measure, but you'll need to do it to maintain excitement in your church. In time, when your church is much larger, you may be able to draw great talent from your own congregation, but until that time, you'll need to draw from other sources.

You have to balance between entertainment and inspiration. There's usually an element of entertainment in most exciting church services, but it should not be the primary purpose of the service. Don't reject entertainment, but don't make it the core of your church.

Surely one or two among these ten methods will help you build excitement. It will be worth your best efforts. Nothing is more exciting than unsaved people coming to your church and being won to the Lord.

■ STEP 8 ■
LAUNCH A GROWTH THRUST

Launch a vigorous growth thrust aimed toward breaking the barrier. People love the excitement of growth and the conversion of new people. It's important to take advantage of that excitement and to get through the barrier while the *pioneers* and *power structure* are rejoicing in the spiritual victories so much that they don't realize what's happening to the fellowship patterns, leadership roles, and styles of ministry. Launching a vigorous growth program is critical to barrier-breaking.

When you set up a vigorous growth plan, schedule it so it begins in the fall or spring, not in summer or winter, unless those are the growth seasons in your locale. Pull out all the stops, and whatever you plan for growth, choose methods that are growth-effective.

In planning a growth thrust, ask yourself these four questions:

1. *What program will appeal to the largest number of people?* While some specialization is effective, you don't want to over-segment. If you target too small an audience, you'll be hard pressed to secure the response you desire. This is especially true in small communities.

2. *What's the capability of your church?* Choose a program the church has the workers and facilities to operate effectively. Don't bite off more than you can chew!

3. *What's especially attractive to people at this time?* In other words, what's "hot" in the culture right now? Good timing is a terrific advantage. At the same time, consider the long-term possibilities of the program. You don't want to launch a program that very few people will be interested in 12 months from now.

4. *What can the church get enthusiastic about?* A growth thrust needs to be attractive and exciting. It needs to be

something that will stir the imagination of people—something that will cause them to hope for great things.

I suggest four growth program categories for consideration.

A. *Children's Ministry*

Year after year the most receptive people to the church are parents of young children. The desire to provide religious instruction for their children is undoubtedly the major motivation that causes them to turn to the church. This may be cultural overhang because of the history of Christianity in North America. On the other hand, it may simply be parental instinct in seeking to instill ethical foundations for good citizenship. Whatever the motivation, pastors of growing churches report that providing a first-class children's ministry program is one of the most effective outreach tools the church has in today's world.

The operative word in the foregoing sentence is "first-class." Second-rate children's programs are not attractive and are, in fact, detrimental to growth. And "first-class" doesn't necessarily mean prohibitively expensive. The key is good-quality workers. Clean facilities and equipment are essential, but they don't have to be the latest thing in the industry.

The best and most accessible space in the building should be given to this program. If possible, a full- or part-time director should be engaged. If you've selected the right person, he or she will figure out how to get the facilities updated and secure the number of volunteer workers that will be required. There's always lots of untapped money and service in local churches.

Properly selecting the volunteer workers and providing ongoing training will keep the program effective for years. Background checks are essential in these days. Failing to make them is setting the church up for disaster.

Loving, caring, capable workers can be every bit as effective as professional workers. There is an abundance of materials and ideas for children's workers. Large churches share freely with smaller churches striving to improve their ministries. Most churches over 100 are capable of establishing a solid children's ministry program that can expand and grow with the congregation.

B. *Congregational Satisfaction Development*

It's generally agreed that word-of-mouth advertising is the best. Satisfied customers not only return but bring others with them. In the church, people who are happy with the church and excited about its ministries are likely to tell their friends and neighbors. We know from widespread research that an invitation to church from a family member, friend, or associate is the way approximately 80 percent of people come to church—and to Christ!

Creating a congregation of people who are excited about the church is not an easy task. It certainly requires more than *telling* the people to be excited—although even that's worth a try! The development of an enthusiastic and excited pride in the church is the result of a church doing a lot of things right. The church must become a place to which people are not only willing but eager to invite their friends.

Many Christians love their church and its leadership but would be embarrassed for a friend or associate to visit, fearing he or she would think less of them for attending a church like that. Unless, and until, a church can overcome those feelings on the part of their people, there's little hope of activating them in outreach ministries.

The easiest place for a church to begin is at its building. Most churches need more than paint—though that would improve many buildings. To visit many churches is to enter a time warp. The design, furnishings, and arrangements are from the 1950s and 1960s. In many cases the furnishing are in good repair, but they just look strange. It's difficult to think of replacing furnishings that are "perfectly good." They may be strong and clean, but they're not "perfectly good." They shout to the world that the church is out of date. Probably not one person in the congregation would be seen in public wearing clothes from the '50s or '60s. Yet church boards will discuss for endless hours the wisdom of spending money to replace things that are in perfectly good condition. Of course, frugality is good, but it may be destructive to the outreach capability of the church. I say "may be" because buildings are only one part of developing excitement about the church.

Let's move from the easiest to the most difficult. Competency in appropriately leading an effective worship service will be the greatest challenge. It will also make the most difference in people's attitude about the church. Most pastors are highly educated and quite intelligent people. Many, if not most, are good in personal relationships. Unfortunately, most have not perceived the crucial importance of how a worship service is directed. Several qualities are important.

- **Appearance.** Casual or formal, it's important to appear impeccably groomed. A "bad hair day" just won't pass in the pulpit. People of the congregation want to be proud of their pastor. It's an honor of inestimable value that people feel that way about their pastor.

- **Attitude.** A pastor must go to the platform with a positive optimistic attitude. It will show through in every thing the pastor does from singing with the congregation to making the announcements, preaching the sermon and, yes, receiving the offering! A person who is positive and optimistic is attractive even before he or she says a word. God is so great, the call to ministry is such an honor, and most churches hold their pastor in such high esteem that any pastor should feel great about standing between heaven and earth for the people in the church. Sure, there are problems; yes, there are criticisms; and certainly there are heartaches in ministry. But for one short time frame on Sunday morning the pastor should, by God's grace, rise above it and revel in the majesty of serving at the sacred desk!

- **Grace.** Paul talks about letting your words be "seasoned with salt." Heed your words. Make them like "apples of gold in baskets of silver." The very sound of your voice should bring comfort and inspiration to your people. Crude remarks, poor grammar, pointless humor, rambling announcements, thoughtless references, and unkind insinuations should be avoided like the plague. In instances in which you deal with issues of judgment and retribution, it should be with a broken heart and a spirit of love. Remember:

Boys flying kites can haul in those white-winged birds:
But you can't do that when you're flying words. . . .
Thoughts unexpressed may sometimes fall back dead,
But God himself can't kill them when they're said.[1]

- **Competency.** Be the best you're capable of being in the pulpit. Study hard. Prepare diligently. Practice your sermon. Get a competent person to critique your presentation, and listen to him or her without being defensive (yes, I know I'm suggesting the miraculous). Many pastors, perhaps most, never improve as preachers because they assume they're doing well. The tragedy is that they could do so much better if they only knew what to correct. People expect much more from pastors today than they did a generation ago. "Winging it" won't work in today's church. Learn how to direct a service more effectively and how to preach a better sermon, and your people will love you for it. And they will, with pride, invite their friends to visit their church.

Perhaps you understand now why I said this is the most difficult task. Actually, this is only the beginning. Much more is involved in securing congregational satisfaction and enthusiasm about the church than pastoral improvement. Significant improvement in programs and congregational culture is equally necessary. Perhaps you're thinking that it's just too much, that there's no way you can accomplish such a miraculous change in the church. It may seem impossible, but with effort and persistence, it's achievable.

In the following chapter I'll contend for placing the priority on quantitative growth during the growth thrust. The purpose is not to elevate quantity above quality. The issue is timing. When is the right time to put the emphasis on quantity, and when is the appropriate time to emphasize quality?

If you decide to engage in congregational satisfaction development, a focus on quality will be essential. It will, in fact, also be a quantitative thrust, for the purpose in a qualitative improvement in the church will be to win people to the church and to Christ.

Of course, there needs to be improvement in programs. Christian education, group life, fellowship, music, community service, and other programs need to be improved as much as possible. A significant change in congregational attitude toward new people will be one of the most productive improvements the church can make.

The best way to begin improvement in congregational attitude toward new people is by helping them understand the evangelism process. Most congregations assume people should first believe and then belong. In fact, it's coming to belong that precipitates believing. It's now fairly clear that decisions for Christ made outside an existing network of Christians don't usually endure. When a congregation comes to understand and accept this fact, it's then possible to help them see how they can change in their attitudes and actions toward new people. If the process is developed in an atmosphere and structure of prayer, people may be willing to participate in programs that facilitate the reception of new people. Prayer also enables people to develop a positive and optimistic attitude, which is so important to the overall spirit of the congregation.

   C. *Multiple Programming (all kinds of groups—not necessarily small)*

We've known for years that everything big is made of little pieces. Large churches are composed of multiple small groups. Traditionally, the groups have been Sunday School classes. Growth-minded pastors have developed large Sunday Schools by multiplying classes. Today many churches promote small-group Bible studies, small-group prayer cells, small-group task forces, special-interest small groups, and a plethora of other kinds of small groups.

There are many theories concerning small groups and the way to make them most effective. Which theory you adopt may depend on both contextual and institutional factors in your church. For the present discussion, the primary consideration is the multiplication of groups. As the number of active groups increases, the number of people attending the church will also increase.

Small groups require leadership. You'll be able to multiply groups only as you train competent leaders. An ongoing leader development program must be established. Small groups have a high infant mortality rate and a limited life expectancy. There will be constant turnover in leaders and participants. Groups will "wax and wane." A long-term commitment to group ministry will be essential in order to realize growth from group multiplication.

Task groups and special-interest groups usually enjoy the longest term. Because they have a focus on a particular activity like sports, hobbies, or projects, they're able to maintain their vitality longer than groups focused on fellowship and study. But many good books on groups are available. You'll need to choose what seems best in your situation. Just remember: if you use groups as a growth thrust, you must keep the emphasis on multiplication.

D. *Radical Outreach*

In stressing the ways of launching a growth thrust, I want to suggest serious consideration of George G. Hunter's appeal in his powerful book *Radical Outreach: The Recovery of Apostolic Ministry and Evangelism.* Dr. Hunter is convinced that only about 1 percent of North American churches are growing by the conversion of pre-Christian people. With 80 percent of the churches stagnant or declining, the remainder of churches are increasing from biological growth and transfer growth.

For the most part, churches have given up on "impossible people." Dr. Hunter's identification of them is potent: "In broad categories, there are two kinds of people who the typical traditional church never engages and invites: (1) those not "refined" enough to feel comfortable with us and (2) those whose lives are too out of control, or too different from ours, for us to feel comfortable with them."[2]

These two categories include the majority of unchurched people in most communities. They're a vast potential outreach for the church. But the traditional church will have difficulty in reaching them. "When seekers come to church, they are often asking two questions: (1) 'Is this faith for people like me?' and (2) 'Do any people like me go to this church?'"[3] To be able to effectively incorporate these people will require such great congregational change that it's an unlikely achievement for most churches. However, that's an inadequate reason for not seeking to reach them. New churches, filled with contemporary-minded young people, may be highly effective in reaching these people if they use the right strategies. Existing churches can, should, and must sponsor new congregations for the purpose of reaching these people. Of course, some congregations have the capability of becoming a church that can reach "impossible" people. In such situations serious consideration should be given to launching a growth thrust to these pre-Christian populations.

If a church gets it right about the "launch a growth thrust" step, they have a very good chance of generating rapid growth and breaking through the 200 barrier.

■ STEP 9 ■
EVANGELIZE FIRST

Break the barrier! Flood the church with new people, and work on consolidation afterward. You may think you need to have all your consolidation programs in place before you break the barrier, but you won't be able to do that. Go for growth! Turn all your energies toward getting scores of people from your prospect list into the church. Enroll them in your group-life structure and in your Sunday School. After that, you can train workers, bring stronger leaders into the system, expand the staff, enlarge facilities, and proliferate programs around the scores of new people.

Across the years I've been told we need to educate our people in how to win souls and to disciple them so they'll be spiritually capable of winning a soul. That makes sense, and I believed it for several years, but it finally dawned on me that education seldom produces evangelism. Rather, evangelism makes education necessary. You can train people, educating and discipling them for years, but that won't motivate them to actually win a soul to Christ. As Dan McBride's paro-dy[4] about soul winning so humorously says,

We've all read a book by Truett.

Now we know how,

But we still won't do it.

That's what you're up against. People will learn how to be soul winners but never go and win souls.

Church growth is messy. If you evangelize and win new converts into your church, you'll be forced to educate them. When people see that new converts need support and recovery groups, they'll begin to call for those ministries. When they begin talking about their lifestyle in the fellowship groups, people are going to say, "We must get something going for these new converts. We need to train these folk in Christian ethics. They need to know the Bible better. We must have Christian development classes for them."

The existence of new converts gives you a reason to train. Becoming a better disciple doesn't adequately motivate you to go out and make new converts. So it's important to flood the church with new people and then convert and disciple them. If you don't, you'll lose them. It's time to develop group life, train workers, expand staff, enlarge facilities, and proliferate programs when you have a significant increase in people.

The dynamic tension between evangelism and education will fuel the quantity-versus-quality argument. There's much to be said in favor of quality. The very nature of Christianity favors an emphasis on quality. The redeeming work of Christ and the holiness of God appeal for quality. Increasing in size usually generates interest in quality, and church members who six months earlier were excited about quantity suddenly become interested in quality. The old adage "Anything worth doing is worth doing right" begins to be frequently heard.

Certainly a church should offer good-quality services, as

we've explained in the previous chapter. But it's often difficult to simultaneously generate both quality and quantity. The pursuit of quality expends energy that could be spent in increasing quantity.

There may be something in the very nature of quality that tends to militate against quantity. Regardless of the tension, the priority must be on quantity when the church is trying to get through the 200 barrier as rapidly as possible. Unless the focus is on quantity, there really won't be any additional growth on which to improve quality. Opportunity to improve quality will come in due time.

There will be people in the congregation who simply can't accept any priority other than quality. This conflict will be expressed in a variety of ways, but growth must be gained while it's possible and in sufficient numbers to carry you through the barrier.

Another aspect of keeping the priority on evangelism will be the tension between growth and morale. Does growth produce morale, or does morale produce growth? There's general agreement that if you have good morale, almost anything you do will work. Conversely, if you don't have good morale, much of what you attempt will be unsuccessful. It's easier to create growth than morale, and even if morale is generated, it will be fragile unless it's supported by growth. Morale is the heady feeling one gets from the sweet smell of success. "Nothing succeeds like success." A growing church will create morale, and morale will generate growth.

Balancing these tensions is an important part of flooding the church with people and then trying to consolidate the gains. The emphasis must be kept on growth, quantity, and evangelism while not completely disregarding morale, quality, and education. The idea is not to ignore discipling but to prevent it from weakening the evangelistic effort. There should be a plan for starting new groups as the church wins new people. The same is true for enlarging facilities and expanding programs as growth occurs.

Step 9 in summary is this: Focus your efforts on winning people rather than pursuing other activities with the hope that they'll win people. Evangelize first, since it's easier to get the church to accept growth plans when it's actually growing. Flood the church with new people, and then intensify your consolidation efforts after you've broken the barrier.

8
LEADING

■ STEP 10 ■
LEAD THE CHANGE

The pastor must be a change agent, not just in the revolutionary sense but in development and in coordination and control of balance in the organization while it undergoes change. It's frequently said, "Pastor, you're the key." Anytime we want to get right down to rock-bottom responsibility, we declare it's all a matter of leadership. Perhaps it's an oversimplification to say that success depends on the pastor, but it does highlight the critical importance of the church's human leader.

A growth-oriented pastor has the ability to organize and administer the church so that the focus is on outreach and evangelism and on meeting the needs of people. It isn't necessarily that he or she is a gifted singer or preacher, although both of those may figure significantly, nor is it that he or she has a winsome personality. It's rather that he or she has a knack for coordinating growth, for connecting with people and meeting their needs, for making sure the things that need to happen in the congregation actually happen.

As I visit churches, I sometimes hear a growth-oriented pastor say, "Excuse me a minute," as he or she picks up the phone and calls someone. I'll hear him or her say something like this: "Will you check on Charles and Mary? Is someone going to be picking them up for the service, or is someone going to be taking a meal over there to them?" What this pastor is doing is taking care of the needs of the people in that congregation. If you ask him or her how important details like that are to growth, he or she will probably say they're not very important. Instead, this pastor will tell you that he or she prays a lot. He or she will tell you of the importance of focusing on great public services. But the facts are, this pastor instinctively knows that people's needs must be met, and he or she makes sure those needs are taken care of. That's real church growth leadership—the kind a pastor must provide if he or she is to pilot the church through the changes necessary to break the 200 barrier. At least six concepts are involved in giving leadership to this kind of change.

1. *You must have a firm resolve to change regardless of the price.* If you don't have that kind of commitment, you'll discover the price is too high, and you'll back off. You must be firmly convinced that the church must change from the ingrown concept of an exclusive family to an evangelistic organization—not to satisfy anyone's ego but that souls will be saved. Change may be the only alternative if you're going to evangelize your community. Make a firm resolve to change.

2. *Realize that all change is perceived as pain.* Until I realized this fact of human nature, I had a lot of trouble with people who didn't want to change. I loved change, especially when people were changing to fit my preferences. It took me a long time to learn that *all* change is painful. Not all change brings the same degree of pain, but it's still painful, and you have to understand that to control it. People are not just hardheaded, resisting change because they're traditionalists. Rather, it's the fact that you've created great discomfort in their lives. If they could be objective about it, the way you are, it wouldn't bother them, but they can't. They're human

beings, and you've torn up something that was very comfortable for them, and they're in pain.

3. *Keep the people willing to endure the pain for the gain.* Say to them, "I know this is very inconvenient for you, but we're doing it for Jesus' sake. We're winning souls. Here are Bob and Helen Carlisle, who were saved last week in their homes because you made this sacrifice."

In one of my pastorates we had Sunday School classes in a building nearly 200 yards away. I had to constantly say to those people, "Thank you for going to that other building for Sunday School class. I know it would have been much easier to stay here in the comfort of this building, but we're able to reach many more people because of your willingness to inconvenience yourselves." My gratitude was sincere. My people were willing to endure the pain for the gain. To keep the goal before them lessens the pain. Spiritualize the goal, and celebrate the victories.

4. *Lead the thrust to reach new people.* One of the most important aspects of controlling the change is the pastor's leadership. After the barrier has been broken, he or she can modify his role somewhat, but until significant growth actually occurs, the pastor must lead the thrust and be a fellow worker with the people.

5. *Take care of people.* See that prospects are visited and drawn into a group circle. Introduce intentionality into the entire social incorporation aspect of the evangelism process. Don't wait for visitors and prospects to find friends. Create settings in which it will happen easily. People aren't looking for a friendly church—they're looking for a friend.

6. *Expand the organization and administration to make continued growth possible.* This requires more staff, more groups, more programs, more ministries, more training, more facilities. One of the reasons we encounter numerical barriers

is that we assume, since the organization and administration we've had in the past have served us well, they'll also be good enough for the future. That's a faulty assumption. We must constantly keep expanding the organization. Some of the fastest-growing churches in North America start a new ministry almost weekly. Think of that!

Growing churches generally add a new staff member for every 100 people. Someone may ask, "Won't we ever get done?" Not as long as you're growing. People will complain that they're out of breath. They probably always will be, but if you stop to catch your breath, you'll stop growing. If you're going to keep growing, you must keep expanding.

You may say, "We won 50 new converts last year. Do we have to win 60 this year?" Yes, if you want to grow. And probably next year it'll be 70. You say, "There's a limit to what I can do." That's right. And each has to find his or her own limit, what he or she is willing to do, and what his or her vision is. That's in the law of things. You're either growing or you're dying. The Lord be thanked—there *are* ways of growing.

The point I'm trying to make is that the pastor must give leadership to all this change—the change from being restricted to an exclusive family kind of church to becoming an outward-looking organization that can ensure that a complex variety of congregational needs are met. This is as important from a functional point of view as praying is from a spiritual point of view. Leadership generates, integrates, and facilitates growth to a remarkable extent. The pastor who plans for his or her church to break the 200 barrier must give thought and commitment to his or her own leadership development.

CONCLUSION
YOU CAN!

If you're not now saying, "I've never been more enthusiastic about breaking the 200 barrier in my church—I can't wait to get started on the steps outlined in this book," you're probably somewhere between that position and one that says, "I've read through these 10 steps, and I believe in the concepts presented—but I don't feel I have the gift of faith or the ability to overcome my own and my church's inadequacies. The hurdles are too high and too many to break the 200 barrier!"

Wherever you fall between those two attitudes, I want to encourage you to go for it anyway. Making an attempt is in itself a step toward success. The illustrious Teddy Roosevelt declared, "Far better it is to dare mighty things, to win glorious triumphs, even though checkered by failure, than to take rank with those poor spirits who neither enjoy much nor suffer much, because they live in the gray twilight that knows not victory nor defeat."

That's especially true in the work of God's kingdom. Any spiritual venture requires that we trust God for enablement, whatever our gifts or abilities. The truth is that you can lead your church in breaking the 200 barrier. You won't coast through it, and you won't slip through it, but at this point you will have already committed yourself to intensive, intentional effort. And if your church is in the 100-150 category, you probably have all the material and human resources necessary.

The factors leading to growth are elusive. Though generally explained in terms of leadership, identifying the characteristics of leadership is almost as difficult as explaining growth. Many are convinced that a person either is born with leadership qualities or else will never have them. That may be true of most great leaders, but there's also evidence that such qualities can be developed. Great gifts of leadership are not so important as enthusiasm, persistence, and attention to detail. You can manage these.

The information on "choice points" also needs to be factored into the equation. While leadership is certainly important, it now appears that congregational culture is equally crucial to growth that will break the 200 barrier. Give careful attention to the educational process that will help liberate your congregation from the growth-restricting results of improperly responding at significant choice points.

The pastor who intends to lead the church through the 200 barrier must be ready to settle for hard work, but a buoyant spirit will go a long way toward lightening the load. In this assignment, vibrancy of spirit is needed, and it will come as you see the evidence of God's moving in response to your plans and prayers. If the pastor must force himself or herself to be optimistic and to act enthusiastically, then God will help him or her to do that too. Optimism, enthusiasm, and spiritual vigor will be integrated into a radiance that will appeal to those who observe what's happening.

The barrier will not be broken overnight. There will be setbacks. It will sometimes look impossible. But if you refuse to be discouraged and persistently pursue your goal, you'll almost certainly overcome the obstacles and experience success.

Persistence will be more than just hanging on. It will be an attention to detail that ensures that the job will get done and the goals will be reached. This need not become a laborious involvement in "administrivia," but it must include a regular checking of all the factors that require attention in the growth process. The pastor may not be directly involved in the performance of these responsibilities, but he or she must see that those who are so involved actually get the job done. People often don't do what's expected, but they usually do what's *in*spected. Make certain that tasks related to growth get done.

The 10 steps to breaking the 200 barrier, with their many subparts, in conjunction with choice points training may appear very complex, but the task is certainly manageable. It's a bit like building a grandfather clock. A scary presentiment rattles your self-confidence around as you look at the picture of the finished product, but each part, put in its place separately and in order, makes the task manageable.

You can do it. Go for it!

Remember free resources are available at <www.200barrier.org>.

NOTES

Chapter 1

1. Cited in *International Encyclopedia of the Social Sciences,* ed. David L. Sills (New York: Macmillan Co. and the Free Press, 1968), 134.

2. J. Alan Winter, *Continuities in the Sociology of Religion* (New York: Harper and Row, 1977), 110-11.

3. Kenneth E. Crow, *What Are Choice Points?* unpublished paper, 2004, 1.

4. Ibid.

5. Kenneth E. Crow, *A Network of Congregations: Congregation Size,* unpublished paper, 2004, 2.

Chapter 2

1. Donald McGavran, *The Bridges of God* (New York: Friendship Press, 1955), 109-12.

Chapter 3

1. John C. Maxwell, *How to Break the 200 Barrier Seminar Notebook: Developing the Type of Leadership and Congregation Needed to Break the 200 Barrier,* May 1987, 1-5.

Chapter 4

1. Malcolm Gladwell, *The Tipping Point* (Boston: Little, Brown and Co., 2000), 175-85.

Chapter 6

1. C. Peter Wagner, *How to Break the 200 Barrier Seminar Notebook: Breaking the 200 Barrier,* May 1987, 8-9.

2. Maxwell, *How to Break the 200 Barrier Seminar Notebook,* 1.

3. George G. Hunter III, *Radical Outreach: The Recovery of Apostolic Ministry and Evangelism* (Nashville: Abingdon Press, 2003), 105-6.

4. Carl F. George, *How to Break the 200 Barrier Seminar Notebook: Shepherds and Ranchers,* May 1987, 1.

5. C. Peter Wagner, *Strategies for Growth* (Ventura, Calif.: Regal Books, 1987), 26.

6. John C. Maxwell, *How to Break the 200 Barrier Seminar Notebook: How to Mobilize Your Laity to Break the 200 Barrier*, May 1987, 2-4.

7. Gene Grate, *Real Life Resources*, <www.realliferesources.org>.

8. Louis A. Allen, *Professional Manager's Guide* (Palo Alto, Calif.: Louis A. Allen Associates, 1977), 127.

9. Ram Charan, *What the CEO Wants You to Know* (New York: Crown Business, 2001), 17-55.

10. *The U.S. Congregational Life Survey*, supported by the Lily Endowment Inc., the Louisville Institute, and the Research Services office of the Presbyterian Church (USA) was conducted in April and May 2001. Deborah Bruce, Cynthia Woolever, and Keith Wulff directed this survey of nearly 300,000 worshippers in the United States.

Chapter 7

1. Will Carelton, "The First Settler's Story," cited in Boyd K. Packer, "Balm of Gilead," *Ensign*, November 1987, 16-17

2. Hunter III, *Radical Outreach*, 43.

3. Ibid., 91-92.

4. Dan McBride, *CHM 58 LP Recording: Tiptoe Through the Tithers*, Dallas: CHM Recordings, n.d.